The Shift to JIT

The Shift to JIT
How People Make the Difference

Ichiro Majima

Productivity Press

CAMBRIDGE, MASSACHUSETTS

NORWALK, CONNECTICUT

Originally published as *JIT kakumei* by Nikkan Kōgyō Shimbun, Ltd., Tokyo © 1988.

English translation copyright © 1992 by Productivity Press, Inc.
Translated by Warren Smith.

Productivity Press
P.O. Box 3007
Cambridge, Massachusetts 02140
United States of America
Telephone: (617) 497-5146
Telefax: (617) 868-3524

Book and cover design: Gary Ragaglia
Printed and bound by: Bookcrafters
Printed in the United States of America
Printed on acid-free paper.

Library of Congress Cataloging-in-Publication Data

Majima, Ichirō, 1938-
[JIT kakumei. English]
    The shift to JIT: how people make the difference/Ichiro Majima
    translated by Warren Smith.
    p.   cm.
    Translation of: JIT kakumei : shikakenintachi no kiroku.
    Includes bibliographical references and index.
    ISBN 0-915299-93-3
    1. Just-in-time systems — Japan.   I. Title.
TS157.M3213 1982   91-42521
658.5'6 — dc20   CIP

Contents

Publisher's Message

While numerous books have been written about Japan's manufacturing prowess, I can't think of a single work that has described the Japanese experience like the book you hold here. Indeed, while my colleagues and I have published dozens of volumes about Japanese manufacturing and management techniques, no Japanese authority has come forth to describe the JIT experience as has Ichiro Majima. In every respect, *The Shift to JIT: How People Make the Difference* is a unique book.

The author is one of Japan's most respected business journalists and has been in the forefront of reporting on the evolving manufacturing revolution in his country. As editor-in-chief of Japan's premier Japanese manufacturing journal, *Factory Management* (*Kōgyō kanri*), Ichiro Majima has spent the past two decades covering such topics as just-in-time (JIT), worksite improvement, and factory rationalization campaigns.

This particular book is unprecedented. *The Shift to JIT* is a learned journalist's view of how a cross-section of Japanese companies has approached the implementation of Toyota production methods, including JIT techniques, *kanban*, and the 5S's, into their own workplaces — sites and circumstances that differ from one another as do night and day. Let's not forget that Japanese companies are as different from each other as are their Western counterparts, making for a fascinating — if not infinite — set of possible variables.

This is what first attracted Majima's attention following the 1973 oil shock that rocked the world's economic stability. Regardless of a company's specific requirements, JIT not only seemed to accomplish something close to miraculous but its precepts were also simple if not paradoxical to common practice — to produce only what is needed, only when it is needed, and only in the quantity needed. In the age of mass production, how could such a concept be the answer? Majima was hooked. He visited company after company, inter-viewing workers and floor supervisors, plant managers and senior executives, and the great Japanese manufacturing geniuses — men like Taiichi Ohno, Shigeo Shingo, Hiroyuki Hirano, Kenichi Sekine, and Tōmō Sugiyama, all of whom had a love affair with the factory floor.

Majima reported his findings in issue after issue of *Factory Management* and what he found astounded him. Readers worldwide hounded him for more information. The manufacturing success stories he witnessed were amazing, but no less amazing was the fact that many Japanese companies didn't — and still don't — practice JIT. Just-in-time could be called a management theory, but more so it is a practical theory based on the workplace itself. JIT cannot happen from management offices. JIT happens in the workplace itself — on the manufacturing floor, in the assembly lines, at the subcontractor, even in clerical offices — because JIT puts people first. People make the difference — not ivory tower thinkers and dreamers, but real operators, floor supervisors, and plant managers;

men and women alike, part-time and salaried workers, inexperienced novices, and veterans of the work force. JIT is based on the involvement of real people in real workplaces at work on real products.

This, of course, is where many companies fail. Their executives think that corporate goals based on JIT principles will produce JIT results. But unless a company involves every person in the process, unless the company truly believes in the creative ability of individual employees, unless company attitudes make everyone a "team player" — JIT cannot flower.

Because of his fascination with the JIT process and its possibilities, Majima dogged the footsteps of Japan's leading JIT consultants as they traveled around Japan, the Pacific Rim, America, and Europe. Every situation differed. And while JIT concepts may be simple and make common sense, applying them demands a lot of hard work — and I mean the roll-up-your-sleeves, dirt-under-the-fingernails type. Each chapter in this book tells the compelling story of a different company and how it dealt — or failed to deal — with its particular challenges. Not every company was successful. For some of them, resistance to change, labor union problems, socio-cultural behavior, and so forth were too great. Every story is amazingly informative as we can't help but see ourselves reflected in the ongoing dilemmas. These factory floors breathe and, in some instances, even sing with innovation and motivation. People first. JIT is not about machines — it is about people.

The Shift to JIT is made up of three parts and fifteen chapters, a working glossary of commonly used JIT terms, and a selected bibliography.

In Part I, JIT takes Japan by storm, and the eight chapters report on eight companies. Chapter 1 chronicles the evolution of Sunwave Industries, how it went from the brink of collapse and bankruptcy in 1964 (when it was Japan's leading maker of stainless steel sinks) to successfully apply JIT under Hiroyuki Hirano and the JIT Research Group's tutelage. Today Sunwave is a leading manufacturer of made-to-order kitchen systems.

Chapter 2 tells the story of Akita Shindengen Industries, a producer of semiconductor components, and how it came to win Japan's coveted productive maintenance "PM Prize" in 1988. The focus is (1) on how TPM is an indispensable part of JIT and (2) on how Shindengen's president (a people-oriented person) motivated his workers. The moral is that without an "Awareness Revolution" among employees at all levels, JIT techniques will not progress.

Matsushita Electric Works is perhaps the only company in the world with such a large-scale, complex line of integrated products pertaining to electrical work and the manufacture of electrical equipment and residential construction materials and equipment. Chapter 3 describes how the Ise factory became the company's leading proponent of JIT.

In 1983, Yasuda Industries, a machine tools manufacturer, brought in a consulting company to raise clerical and management efficiency through MRP. The program failed. In 1986, a JIT Research consultant was invited to institute a companywide JIT program. Chapter 4 tells how JIT prevailed over worker resistance.

Chapter 5 tells the story of Shindengen Industries' Okabe plant, a producer of hybrid IC's (integrated circuits) for electrical equipment and semiconductor devices, electrical equipment for two- and four-wheeled vehicles, electrical switching equipment for personal computers, and so on. After experiencing some success in shortening lead times in some areas of the factory, they decided to institute a companywide program.

Chapter 6 tells a fascinating story of how a small subcontractor is affected by JIT. Miyamoto Manufacturing produces compressors for automobile air conditioners and is a 100 percent subcontractor for the Sawa factory, one of the twenty Hitachi factories responsible for generating profits. Aware that Sawa was implementing JIT, Miyamoto's president resolved to do likewise.

In 1983, Tateshina Manufacturing Works, a maker of high-end furniture and a woodworking subcontractor, was unable to meet its parent company's demand to cut costs. Chapter 7 tells the story of their improvement program.

In 1984, the JIT Research Group was asked to provide a new service — to perform a group consultation for five companies in the city of Yonezawa. With overviews of each company, Chapter 8 tells what ensued.

In Part II, Majima follows JIT overseas. Chapter 9 examines Mitsubishi Trading Company's strategy for exporting JIT and then accompanies three Japanese JIT consultants on a tour of Canada and the United States. Chapter 10 records the observations of the Japanese JIT consultants at Renault, Ltd. in France — an uneasy, albeit fascinating learning experience that brought mixed JIT results. In Chapter 11, Korea's thirst for knowledge precipitated an invitation to guide JIT implementation at Samsung Electronics.

Part III presents the author's final synthesis of the JIT wisdom gleaned from the preceding field studies. Chapter 12 emphasizes that JIT's lifeblood is the workplace. With this focus, the author talks about the approaches of Ohno, Shingo, and Sugiyama. Chapter 13 discusses Kenichi Sekine and the JIT "high diversity" research group he leads, their activities and results. Chapter 14 posits that JIT puts people first. Here, the author examines Ohno's philosophy and Toyota's subsequent management training system. Chapter 15 studies methods for promoting a JIT "Awareness Revolution."

Many fine people made this English edition possible. I gratefully acknowledge Mr. Hajime Kitamura, director of the

Publication Division, Nikkan Kōgyō Shimbun, Ltd., for allowing us to produce this book in English. I also personally extend my thanks to Warren Smith, translator; Cheryl Rosen, acquisitions and project editor; Dorothy Lohmann, managing editor; Ron Bridenthal, free-lance copyeditor; Jennifer Cross, proofreader; Elisa Abel, indexer; Gary Ragaglia, cover designer; and the production team of Susan Cobb and Caroline Kutil.

Norman Bodek
President
Productivity, Inc.

Preface

The year 1990 is a year that should truly grieve people involved in the manufacturing field. For this is the year in which two giants successively passed away.

Taiichi Ohno, the father of the Toyota Production System and former vice president of the Toyota Motor Company, died on May 28, 1990. On November 14, Shigeo Shingo, the man who served a very important role as a consultant during JIT's formative period, also died. Without the efforts of these two men Japan's manufacturing industries would not have developed as they have, and Japanese products such as automobiles and home electronics would not be as widely used by people throughout the world as they are today.

Taiichi Ohno originated the just-in-time (JIT) production concept of "supply the market with what is needed when it is needed and in the exact quantities needed." We are indebted to him because the actual result of his work not only turned Toyota into a colossal super company, but also turned Japan into a world class manufacturing power.

Shigeo Shingo greatly influenced Ohno and others during the formative period of Toyota's production system. Besides developing many *kaizen* or improvement techniques, he coined such phrases as "single-minute exchange of die" or SMED, "nonstock production," and "autonomation." At the same time, we could argue that his achievement of widely diffusing Japan's kaizen methods has been more highly lauded in factories abroad than in Japan.

Posthumously, the voices of praise have grown even greater for the illustrious work of these two men. While a great many people mourn their passing, this occasion could also mean our entry into the era of the next generation of research into the production ideals for the twenty-first century. And JIT will most definitely contribute to this new era.

My encounter with JIT was immediately after the first oil shock in 1973. Even now I vividly remember it as having been a shock greater than the circumstances surrounding oil. As a mere journalist who is neither a corporate manager nor a production management researcher, what attracted me most about JIT was its pervasive paradoxical viewpoint. Although all new concepts are paradoxical, I found something fresh in JIT's capacity to embrace the same paradoxes that conventional production management and industrial engineering found themselves altered by.

JIT's fundamental concept of supplying what is needed only when and in the quantities needed is the philosophy of small and large lot production. In other words, the high speed and continuous production of a single product directly conflicted with methods advocating the reduction of cost and lead time. The idea of manufacturing a wide variety of products in only the quantities demanded by the market and utilizing a more flexible system to meet the needs of diverse customers while extracting maximum human ability, experience, and creativity from workers was not accepted in the beginning. Most IE experts and researchers of the time were puzzled by Ohno's philosophy and voiced their opposition.

Regarding production facilities, Ohno has said that a continuous line is either very good or very bad. In most cases, this means that because so many workers are tied up in its operation, problems on a continuous production line are difficult to perceive. On a production line that can be stopped freely, however, problems are brought to the fore. This statement argues in favor of a production line that, because of accumulated improvements, no longer requires stoppages. Such words truly are mixed with irony and hit the truth.

Ohno further states that if people are not put through hardships, their intelligence will not be challenged. This is a paradox that explains that work can be made easier only through the accumulation of repeated effort. He also says that rationalization is achieving the ability to do the ordinary without extra effort. In other words, a rationalized factory appears ordinary. And, indeed, a factory that operates with continuous improvement appears very ordinary, a viewpoint that shares something with the philosophy of Zen.

> *I fully understand what the development of Japan's economy depends on. The content of* The Shift to JIT *is not fabricated and I think people will be surprised by its factuality. I hope that many people grasp its content and put it to practical use.*

These are the thoughts of one reader who read the Japanese version of this book. Yet, even in Japan, the types of companies introduced here are truly few in number. When I wrote this book I endeavored to write the truth as it is. Therefore, the companies and people who appear are all real.

I think that the non-Japanese reader will feel some sense of compatibility with the very different views and methods expounded herein. This is because the companies and consultants presented are rare, even in Japan. My hope is that the shock factor from reading this will be positive — not negative because the roots of Japanese and Western management methodologies are fundamentally different, both historically and structurally.

When European and U.S. companies attempt to introduce JIT and TQC, the so-called Japanese-style management, they frequently encounter problems. This is due to the following reasons:

1. They are impatient for results. They do not establish long-term views or devise means to strengthen the corporate stucture.
2. Theory takes precedence. Actual results and experience are not emphasized.
3. The philosophy of "the customer first" does not filter down from the top to the bottom of the organization.
4. There is insufficient recognition by management of the importance of in-house factory improvement.
5. The Western style of management relies on a demerit system that thrives on criticizing others. In Japan, a merit system avoids blaming others as much as possible.

There are, of course, other examples of differences between the West and Japan in the areas of corporate culture, management style, labor unions, employee involvement, interdivisional communication, education, training, and so on. Nonetheless, I don't believe that these are insurmountable differences that preclude mutual understanding. A lack of agreement between these two systems does not prevent the introduction or implementation of other management methods such as JIT. If we ask what the greatest difference is between the two, I would have to say that it is the difference in attitude toward the customer.

The following vignette concerns the late Konosuke Matsushita, the founder of Matsushita Electric Industries and an exemplary Japanese executive. Once, during a conversation with a Western executive, Mr. Matsushita replied, "No, that is wrong. The customer is a god. Because a king is human, he is capable of mistakes — but a god does not make mistakes."

Most Japanese companies listen carefully to the needs and concerns of their customers and have in place systems that reflect and respond to these needs and concerns. Companies without such systems are unable to survive. This way of thinking extends to every company and to every employee. In other words, companies are putting the most effort into that which is vital to their survival. In *The Shift to JIT*, I wanted to write about the ultimate goal of JIT, which is to respond thoroughly to the needs of the customer.

A strong motivation to write this book was provided by a consultant of very keen sensitivity, and his young and distinguished friends, whom I first met within the pages of the magazine *Kōgyō kanri*, which I have been editing now for many years. My heartfelt thanks go to Hiroyuki Hirano, Naoki Ueno, Kenji Takahashi, and Yūno Gotō of the JIT Management Research Center. And to those enterprises appearing in — and to those I interviewed for — this book, I express my gratitude.

I would like to express my gratitude to the great leaders and pioneers of JIT, the late Taiichi Ohno and Shigeo Shingo. I pray that their souls rest in peace. I also offer my sincere thanks to Norman Bodek, the president of Productivity Press, for giving me the opportunity to have this book published in English.

Without the assistance of Teruo Fukasaku and Kuniaki Kako from the publishing department of the Nikkan Industrial News, this book would not be. These two provided me with courage and strong encouragement to write this book while I was pursuing my regular job.

And finally, nothing would make me happier than if this book was useful to those people who work in manufacturing. This would be an unexpected pleasure for a man who has been "walking the fields" of the workplace magazine industry for twenty-five years.

Introduction

Where Did Japan's Strength Come from and How Long Will It Continue?

"Are you familiar with the *kanban* system?" I first became aware of the Toyota Production System in March 1977 after the first oil shock. A company reorganization had been announced in February, and I would be transferred to the editorial department of *Factory Management* (*Kōgyō kanri*) magazine as of April. Because this would be the first magazine I had ever administered, I took time out to do research. It was then that I was asked the question above, a question to which I could only answer "No." The man who asked me said, "If your magazine deals with making things, then the *kanban* system is the only way to go. What about researching it?"

With that, I made this research an objective. I was overly optimistic in that I thought I would be able to put together a specialty book on the subject in just a short time. At that time, Toyota was very secretive and wouldn't release any details of the system to anybody outside of their plants. Moreover, I couldn't count on people outside of Toyota being able to write about the Toyota Production System.

The first oil shock, which occurred in November 1973, was the greatest blow to Japan since World War II, bringing to a screeching halt the period of high growth that had lasted for ten years. Most companies, including large-scale enterprises, lost sight of even their goals of survival. The damage was especially great to manufacturers. Financial performance caved in. But in the midst of this, not only did Toyota's financial performance not decline, but the company exhibited unwavering corporate strength. The world was amazed — until that time the power of Toyota had not been apparent among the companies that had been lulled to complacency in the period of high growth.

When suddenly companies came to awareness and saw themselves in an era of low or stabilized growth, suddenly there appeared a company called "Toyota," which was towering above them. And when one looked closely at Toyota, one saw a management method, peculiar to Toyota, called (at that time) the "*kanban* system."

Three reasons come to mind as to why the Toyota Production System, which had been in use for twenty years, was unknown to people outside the company and had not been analyzed by outsiders:

1. Toyota itself had made no particular effort to publicize the system. On the contrary, its people made efforts to keep it from the public forum.
2. The system was so different from existing philosophies (in fact, it could be said to be in direct opposition to prevailing philosophies) that no scholars or researchers were willing to champion the issue. Although in 1978 my magazine asked workers about

the production system, most people doubted the methods. Scholarly evaluations of the time were divided.

3. The methods were inelegant, work-floor-based, and thus difficult to evaluate. The concepts were more easily accepted by the practitioners (those on the work floor) than by the thinkers (the engineers and management).

Just-In-Time

In May 1978, the long-awaited *Toyota Production System: Beyond Large-scale Production* (published in English by Productivity Press in 1988) was published. The book was written by Taiichi Ohno, called the father of the Toyota Production System, who was then vice president of Toyota Motors. The book — with its recurring theme of seeking management of simplification — had a great impact on most of the managers who read it. I also recall a shock like being hit over the head with a blunt instrument when I read the book — the issues raised seemed to destroy that which had always seemed to be common sense. The book was that year's best seller.

Since its inception, according to Taiichi Ohno, the Toyota Production System followed the philosophy held during the era of Toyota founders Sakichi and Kiichirō Toyoda of "raising production efficiency through eradicating all types of waste from the company."

> *Summarizing the production system of Kiichiro Toyoda, it is to "manufacture every day that which is needed in the amounts that are needed." When putting this into practice, it is unavoidable that all processes, whether they want to or not, must become assembly line operations. "Just-In-Time" is the Japanese-English that Kiichiro used at the time for the actual English words "Just On Time." Basically, the philosophy was "If it arrives in time, that's good — but don't make any extra." At that time, the system wasn't*

actually a "kanban" system, but instead each morning a bulletin with the production numbers for the day would be circulated. Once the predetermined numbers of parts were produced, then it was all right to go home early. If the numbers were not achieved, however, the result would be having to stay late until they were. When it came to fully establishing the philosophy of assembly line operations, it was of utmost importance to thoroughly train and educate the workers, especially those who would become managers and foremen. Because the system was a radical change, it was first necessary to wipe clean the minds of those who had the old production system stuck in their heads. The training book made by Kiichiro was ten centimeters thick, and assembly line operations were described in great detail. This book was the root for the Toyota Production System. . . . Kiichiro was unable to fully implement the production system, the system that included retraining the workers, because of the start of World War II. It was the postwar responsibility of Vice President Taiichi Ohno to revive and develop the production system using kanban. (From "My Personal History" by Toyota President Eiji Toyoda, a series of articles published by the Japan Economic Times*).*

It was Taiichi Ohno who developed the concepts of the Toyota Production System into methods and corresponding technologies.

There have been many great pioneers in the field of production technology. One of these, Frederick W. Taylor, is the father of scientific management. At the end of the nineteenth century and the beginning of the twentieth, management methods emphasizing efficiency began in the United States and spread throughout the world. According to Taylor, the barriers to manufacturing efficiency were that (1) the workers performed systematic sabotage and (2) the methods used to determine wages were irrational. As ways to rationally and scientifically establish wages, Taylor performed time studies and task management. Through these he was able to establish standard operations and to control the time of production activities based on these criteria, and the concepts of "standardization" were born.

The "Ford System" of Henry Ford mechanized Taylor's time-based control of operations. It was Ford who conceived the conveyer-driven production lines. These production line methods were the driving force behind dramatic improvements in the manufacture of automobiles at the time.

Taiichi Ohno has said, "I think that were the American automobile king Henry Ford alive today, no doubt he would have done the same thing that I have done with Toyota's production system." Ohno evaluates the following points of the Toyota Production System:

> Like Ford's system, the Toyota Production System is based on the assembly line or work flow system. The difference is that, while Charles E. Sorensen, Ford's first president and head of production, worried about warehousing parts, Toyota eliminated the warehouse. There is something I would like you to recall here — "Just-In-Time" is having the parts needed, in the amount and at the time needed.

The following is also written about eradicating waste and about standardization.

> I believe Ford was a born rationalist — and I feel more so every time I read his writings. He had a deliberate and scientific way of thinking about industry in America. For example, on the issues of standardization and the nature of waste in business, Ford's perception of things was orthodox and universal.
>
> We see in Ford's thinking his strong belief that a standard is something not to be directed from above. Whether it be the federal government, top management, or a plant manager, the person who establishes the standard should be someone who works in production. Otherwise, Ford emphasizes, the standard would not lead to progress. And I agree.

There are, however, naturally many areas in which the Ford System and the Toyota Production System do not agree. In the "Toyota Production Technology Lectures" initiated in 1955, the consultant Shigeo Shingo, who came to be in charge of those lectures, compared the Ford System and the Toyota Production System as follows:

- *Large-Lot Manufacturing and Small-Lot Manufacturing.* As opposed to the American-style "anticipate, plan, and forecast" production, the method of the Toyota system is "production to order and production adapting to actual demand through small-lot, short-lead-time production."

- *Mixed Production in the Assembly Process.* While fundamentally the Toyota system utilizes Ford's production line operations, it carries no intermediate inventory. As opposed to the Ford System, which produced a single product in large-lot, small-variety production, the Toyota Production System has a mixed flow of small lots of highly diversified products.

- *Fully Integrated Operations from Parts to Assembly.* As opposed to the Toyota System where there is a single integrated production flow from parts processing to final assembly, the method employed by Ford had operations where there was a single flow only in the final assembly process. In sharp contrast to Toyota, wherein the parts makers and subcontractors engage in one-piece or small lot production, parts fabrication at Ford was done in large lots.

JIT Produces Excellent Products Inexpensively

In markets based on the principles of competition, the main objectives of the manufacturer in any age have always been to make higher quality products less expensively and more quickly. In situations typical of those found before the first oil shock, where the supply cannot keep up with the high demand, if a company could more fully use its resources of people, material, and capital to increase production even slightly, then lower average costs and increased profitability would result.

However, to survive in eras of low growth or in times where markets mature very rapidly, a diversified product line that can respond adequately to changes in demand is necessary simultaneous with offering enticing products demanded by the market, and doing so in a timely manner (with short lead times). Even with products such as automobiles, which are normally thought of as being manufactured in fixed-quantity production systems, an examination of the numbers and types of automobiles sold would reveal that there is data to indicate that of the 19,349 different models available from a particular automobile manufacturer, in a given month half of these models only sell a single vehicle each.

When one reduces the number of car models being produced in a given month, it becomes more difficult to manufacture to forecasts and to sell from inventory; the move to highly diversified, small lot production and make-to-order systems is inevitable — there is no other choice. Production lead times, and the time taken by ordering, production, and sales, must be shortened.

For a company to be profitable, the larger the difference between total sales and total costs, the better. There are only two ways to increase this difference — either to raise the sales prices or to lower the costs. Today's market, however, will not tolerate prices raised according to the whims of manufacturers. Because of this, rather than a "cost-plus pricing system" where an appropriate profit is added to the cost of the product, it is inevitable that profits must derive from a "cost reduction system." Consequently, manufacturing companies must place more emphasis on how inexpensively products can be made.

To make things inexpensively, a company must make high quality products in just the amounts that will sell, using few people and inexpensive equipment. Let's look at an example. If a company hoards several month's worth of materials when just one day's supply would do, or if the company makes 110 units or 120 units because they have some extra workers when they should actually make only 100 units, then the company cannot make the products inexpensively. There will be the need to store these extra materials or manufactured goods, and storage costs come back into the product cost. This is what is meant by saying that costs are determined by those methods by which the products are made.

And the most cost efficient way to manufacture products is — JIT.

JIT Transcends Types of Industry, Scope of Business, and National Boundaries

JIT first spread from the automobile industry where it began into the electronics industry where it was used in similar assembly operations. It later passed into all types of industries, such as the garment industry, food products, restaurants, distribution, and so forth. It has even been used successfully in dry-cleaning shops and recently the Tochigi Prefecture Dairy Farmers Co-op initiated JIT seminars with the goal of gaining a competitive edge.

About ten years ago President Masatoshi Itoh of Itoh Yokado met Taiichi Ohno. The meeting precipitated a JIT revolution in the field of distribution. Just as Toyota had done with its parts suppliers, Itoh Yokado performed "multiple purchasing" and achieved steady success. They were able to actualize both "point of sale" (POS) information control and JIT. All was done in line with consumer needs by stocking on the shelves only goods that would sell, a practice based on the philosophy of getting by without any wasted intermediate inventory. Reportedly, the 7-Eleven group, through implementing POS in their outlets, has been able to reduce the monthly inventory of each store from $30,000 to $20,000. The primary objective in this system was to find the "dead goods" among their inventories. This method contrasts sharply with the U.S. way of finding the saleable goods in inventory. (To read further about Itoh Yokada, refer to Taiichi Ohno's *Just-In-Time for Today and Tomorrow* [Productivity Press, 1988].)

Japan Yūsen is said to be making an American container base camp in Kentucky, implying that it is doing so to service the factory of Toyota America. It appears to be on the verge of creating an ocean-spanning network to provide necessary parts to the necessary locations at the necessary times.

Today JIT transcends all types of industries, all sizes of companies, and national boundaries.

PART ONE

JIT Takes Japan by Storm:
Field Surveys

CHAPTER ONE

Seeing the Light

Sunwave Industries

The JIT General Assembly

April 20, 1988. The first JIT Industrial Committee General Assembly of the JIT Management Research Center was held in the Tokyo Hilton. Although no large companies were represented in the meeting, top management from twenty-three small- and mid-sized companies were in attendance. All of the consultants from JIT Management Research — including Hiroyuki Hirano, Kenji Takahashi, and Yoshimi Gotō — were assembled there, with the exception of Naoki Ueno.

President Kiichi Suyama of Sunwave Industries, representing the corporate members, made the following remarks:

> *Sunwave went into bankruptcy twenty-odd years ago. For a long time, even after its reconstruction, it would not turn a profit. When I assumed the presidency in June 1980, I engaged all my strength and resources, but making improvements was no simple task. Two years ago I entreated the help of Mr. Hirano in renewing JIT in our company, and since last year we have been continually working with JIT.*

In the past few years, products for houses and the housing indus-
tries have changed dramatically. There has been a movement from
stand-alone products to systemized product groups; were we as
manufacturers not to make this transformation, users would not
accept our products. Even if the makers do their best to supply prod-
ucts, if these products are not made according to the demand of the
customers, not a single unit will sell regardless of the sales program.
The old system, that of keeping products in inventory and selling
from there, has become totally obsolete.

In the past I have been responsible for deploying computer sys-
tems and for parts and materials integration (standardization). On
these foundations I base my JIT concept of thoroughly eliminating
waste. Eliminating all waste from management is far more easily
said than done, but by adopting JIT we have established the battle-
ground for the improvement struggle.

Currently my company is being called on television "the com-
pany of the friendly attack," and the more press we have received
from business magazines and the like, the more profitable we have
become. This, too, is a result of JIT.

Bankruptcy

On February 12, 1964, Sunwave Industries asked the Tokyo
District Court to apply the Stock Company Reorganization
and Rehabilitation Act — for all intents and purposes Sunwave was declaring bankruptcy. At that time, Sunwave was
Japan's top maker of stainless steel sinks. After World War II
the company had retooled, had synchronized, and had experienced rapid growth — bankruptcy was inconceivable to the
public and to company employees alike.

The tragedy of Sunwave is that this was the same year that
the country as a whole rallied in the "Olympic economy."
This was the year that the bullet train and the Nagoya-Kyoto
highway were opened and Haneda Airport was linked to the
City of Hamamatsu by monorail. This Olympic economy was
referred to as an economic boom.

Shedding Its Losing Attitude

"After twenty-five years, we still haven't put that experience behind us."

So said President Kiichi Suyama during an interview. To some extent, this comment was typical of Suyama, who although he himself was not directly involved with the incident, knew the sorrow of employees afterward.

Immediately after the bankruptcy, when the ¥2.8 billion stock was reduced by 90 percent, capital was expanded by ¥1.2 billion as a substitute settlement for the restructured debt, resulting in a total capitalization of ¥1.5 billion. Through this the greatest creditor, Nisshin Steel, held between 32 and 35 percent of the company. This arrangement was appropriate because Nisshin Steel was Sunwave's sole supplier for stainless steel.

Suyama was reassigned from his duties at Nisshin Steel to the presidency of Sunwave in 1980 during the worst of the second oil shock. Not only was the external environment unfavorable at that time, but the environment within management was most inhospitable. Morale was low and the company employees lacked motivation.

"There remained the feeling of being a whipped dog. Although we were doing the same things that were making other companies profitable, we just couldn't turn the corner. We felt it essential to thoroughly reform corporate culture." Equipment investments in the factories were low enough to say that they were nonexistent. The company manufactured only low-demand items and had no products with high levels of added value. Suyama's reformation began suddenly in 1982.

The company introduced total quality control (TQC). All employees were asked what should be done to involve everyone in TQC. Answers included introducing an on-line computer system for production control and emphasizing the development of new products and technologies. That same year the company began to use, for the first time, female high school graduates. The focus of life — so new to the company — became the women. To gather the opinions of the women (who were the ultimate users of the kitchen equipment) and to feed these opinions back into management required the utilization of the skills of the women employees. Women were assigned to the development department and to the showroom floors.

Little by little, as more sophisticated products appeared, sales methods changed. Sales could no longer be made by merely dropping products off at the wholesaler's warehouses. It became necessary to monitor customer needs and to tie those needs immediately into product designs. Thus, a computer-aided design (CAD) system was implemented with two objectives in mind: (1) to accelerate the design process through automation, and more importantly, (2) to have the ability to explain our products in detail to customers on the showroom floors in an attempt to fill their needs.

CAD certainly became a strategic tool. The structure of product lines changed, corresponding closely to the needs of the customers. Also, the system enabled the company to determine what it should change next.

The First JIT Revolution

In March 1983 continuing efforts were devoted to the development of an on-line system for the manufacturing department to quickly and inexpensively provide customers with quality products. In August of the same year the system was completed.

Saneakira Yoshino described the system thusly: "Although the thought was to build only that which had been sold, we still followed the production plan that we had made in advance. We had to carry some amount of inventory, and the production control system would order the manufacture of products as the inventory was depleted." Like Suyama, Yoshino came from Nisshin Steel in 1981; he is now the company president's right-hand man. Yoshino is a design engineer with the firm conviction that quality products are destined to sell.

However, the system devised by these men did not work well. Frankly admitting that the concept was poor, Yoshino said,

"Although we were able to make the software, the manufacturing was still being done according to the old system, which couldn't work when you tried to increase its volume. It was a far cry from the system sought by sales that could deliver the right product at the right time in the right amount to the right consumer."

In order to use the software that had been developed, the implementation of JIT began, centering on the data systems department. The Fukugai Works and the wood-working suppliers became involved in the program. Hirano from JIT Research began a three-year JIT implementation in 1983. Kōhei Obinata from the production control department's outside orders section accompanied Hirano on a nationwide JIT pilgrimage.

In a market with decreased demand and no hope for increased consumption, the only choice is to take existing demand away from competitors. More and more consumers demand that products fit their personal preferences. Products that have been special-order products in the past are now becoming regular products, and work floors are being buried with special orders. As the number of product types increases, the only recourse will be first to sell the product, and then to manufacture and deliver it quickly. The most desirable factory is now the one that is efficient and versatile.

Obinata and Hirano discussed the system. Obi began by saying, "Sunwave uses computers as tools to quickly grasp the needs of the market and to accurately transmit that information back to the manufacturing floor. In other words, sales and production have been thoroughly systemized. Were you to draw a comparison to a human body, you have completed the soft matter stored between the ears when you completed this computer system. However, regardless of how much grey matter there is, it is useless unless it is attached to a body. And now the situation is top-heavy and doesn't work."

Hirano continued, "To resolve this situation, the qualities of the manufacturing floor used for mass production must be thought of in an entirely different way — and this is not something easily done. Many people may be unable to catch on to the new way of thinking. Nearly every day will require spending time late into the evening making improvements. First the attitudes of the people will need to be changed, and then the equipment layouts, and after that the production methods — a whole factory revolution."

"Well, to some degree I have resolved myself to that — but where should I begin?"

"Whatever anybody says, the fundamentals for improvements in a company aiming for a factory revolution are the 5S's."

These two people held this sort of dialogue many times. The 5S's are:

- *seiri* — proper arrangement
- *seiton* — orderliness
- *seiketsu* — cleanliness
- *seiso* — cleanup
- *shitsuke* — discipline

Twenty Years' Worth of Inventory Discovered

Companies, like people, accumulate junk over the years. Like cholesterol-choked arteries, unnecessary forms, documents, parts, and products accumulate in the company systems. The "red-tag strategy" is one way to organize this accumulation. Finding the waste and useless junk is a more difficult task, but even more difficult is disposing of it. Even people on the production floor find it difficult to know what inventory is necessary for production and what is not. The approach to JIT begins with exposing the "junk" in the factory — causing the "fat" to rise to the surface.

The red-tag strategy is a method to organize unneeded items using red-colored tags. Anything not used in the production plan for a month (or even a week if the company or factory deems it so) is marked with a red tag. The red tags are put on anything not human — stock, intermediate inventory, products, parts, raw materials, machinery, transportation carts, tools and jigs, tables, chairs, dies, vehicles, fixtures and equipment, and so on. Important points in this tagging process include not being reticent about tagging unused items, but instead tagging them quickly without hesitation; making the tags big so that everyone can see them; designating a place to put the tagged items; knowing the right time to move tagged items; and so forth.

Hirano gave the order, "Make it so that even the company president or factory manager can tell at a glance whether each individual item is used or not."

On February 24, 1983, a section meeting was held within the production control department. The discussion centered on the 5S's. Managing Director Akira Okamura, the production headquarters manager, finally presented the conclusion that a long debate in the meeting had been unable to produce, "OK, let's first tackle the 4S's of proper arrangement, orderliness, cleanliness, and cleaning and create a base for factory improvements. We will designate March '4S Month.'"

On March 1, Okamura's order to execute the 4S's was communicated to all manufacturing complexes and outside suppliers. Red tagging was also emphasized. One factory had estimated at the beginning of the program a need for 500 tags. Once tagging actually began, however, they ended up using 1,500 tags — three times the original estimate.

"But it doesn't make me proud," said Tomonari Maeda, then manager of the Fukugai Works, to Hirano, "No, instead it surprises me. We had twenty years' worth of doors for the system kitchens. It appears as if when one person made a mistake in ordering doors, another said, 'Well, we'll use them eventually,' and accepted the order. The people on the work floor always loudly objected when they ran out of parts, but we had no idea that we had twenty years' worth of inventory."

Maeda described what he had begun to sense for the first time — that the production floor, the people in charge of ordering from suppliers, and the warehousers all looked beyond the mark, feeling that there were no problems as long as there were no stock-outs. The fear was always that the line would stop.

One manufacturing complex did not have enough pallets for materials. When they requested an additional hundred pallets, over 200 were found in the red-tag storage area. The manufacturing complex manager blurted out, "Tomorrow we open a pallet store!" One day the 4S activities went so far that a desk belonging to one of the section managers was marked with a red tag.

To some degree a "visual control system" was created within the factory. People felt that it was a result of the 4S's alone that the inventory level fell by 30 percent in six months and that productivity increased by 20 percent. Obinata looked at his impeccable factory and sensed that soon the curtain would rise on improvements in the workplace.

At this time Sunwave was the first in the industry to develop a totally made-to-order system kitchen, the "Sun Valet." The Fukugai Works was placed in charge of its manufacture. The Sun Valet was an epoch-making product in that it had a lead time of two weeks. Adding the two to three days needed for transportation, the product was planned for delivery to the customer in less than twenty days. It was inconceivable that production could have adapted to these requirements without JIT. For the time being, JIT had paid off.

Yoshino summarizes the first stage of JIT as follows:

> *The reduction in finished-goods inventory in the Fukugai Works was enormous. Although we had to bring in a considerable amount of new equipment for the Sun Valet, the space saved through inventory reduction allowed us to get by without expanding the building. Also, I'm ashamed to say, before JIT we had an inventory turnover rate of only about 0.5 turns per month — that is, we had over two months' worth of raw materials. However, once JIT was initiated, we increased the turns to 2.5 per month. Productivity saw the great increase of 35 percent in one year.*

Furthermore, we located supplier factories throughout the country. In the past, when circumstances became difficult for the suppliers, they immediately increased their unit prices. Soon this stopped and they developed a heightened ambition to assertively improve production.

The first stage of JIT was completed with these excellent results and only a few minor problems. At this time Hirano's involvement with Sunwave came to an end.

The Encounter

Spring 1986. While returning from Hiroshima, President Suyama happened to run into Hirano.

"Mr. President, it's been a long time since we've worked together. How are things going?"

"I'm pleased to say that the factories are doing fine. Lately, however, a growing demand for product modifications requires that we move toward make-to-order manufacturing. Would you come work with us again?"

During JIT's first stage, the only make-to-order product was the Sun Valet produced in the Fukugai Works. However, after 1986 the company's main product had been menu-selected kitchen systems manufactured to customer order.

The second stage of Sunwave's JIT activities, called "S-JIT" for short, began in August of that year. This JIT program had three major themes: (1) to integrate JIT and the "Quality First" philosophies, (2) to introduce JIT to the factory floor and fully establish efficient manufacturing systems, and (3) to develop the human resources in charge of manufacturing, such human resources as the foremen and the improvement staff — in other words, to improve the level of management.

This time the movement was to involve all of the production facilities in three manufacturing complexes, Fukugai, Kiryū, and Heta. The responsibilities and limits to authority of the promotion organization, which in the first stage had been a bit uncertain, this time were clearly defined.

First, the company president was installed as S-JIT promotion headquarters manager, Managing Director Okamura as promotion headquarters assistant manager, Yoshino as promotion office manager, and Obinata as promotion office assistant manager. The promotion committee consisted of the assistant managers of the three manufacturing complexes. The Fukugai Works dispatched one special delegate to the committee as well as twelve middle and floor managers as duty members. The Kiryū Works sent three special delegates and twelve duty members, and the Heta Works sent one special delegate and two duty members.

An all-star consulting cast was assembled — Hirano, Ueno, Gotō, and Takahashi — a line-up that might never be matched again.

Before introducing the Sun Valet, a system kitchen called the "PX" was introduced in the spring of 1981. Although until this time many options were available for each product, the system was designed to mass produce and sell — very different from a make-to-order system. Because of the "mass produce and then sell the product" approach, extreme cases required the company to carry six months of inventory in order to ensure its ability to respond to orders.

"The flaw in trying to apply this same system to Sun Valet," said Yoshimura, "is that we would have to keep about a year's worth of inventory in stock." The interest on a year's worth of dormant inventory would be lost and model changes would be impossible once the inventory had been manufactured.

Fundamentally, S-JIT's aim was to establish a thorough made-to-order production system. Although introducing the computer system was a bit of a detour, with the Sun Valet product the company began to flourish. Following this, the company released an even more sophisticated system, the "Sun Shell."

Introducing the *Kanban* System

The three manufacturing works were divided by the products they produced. The Fukugai Works produced the Sun Valet and the Sun Shell, sophisticated wooden system kitchens. The Kiryū works manufactured gas appliances, porcelain enamel sinks, and porcelain enamel tiles for construction. The Heta Works manufactured industrial galley equipment and stainless steel bathtubs.

The Fukugai Works was ideally situated to implement the *kanban* pull system. The major topic in the Fukugai Works was eliminating "planned production" and making the transition to the *kanban* system, allowing the manufacture of "the right items at the right time in the right amounts."

Every company establishes production plans based on customer demand. However, it is after the production plans are made that the great differences between the "push system" and the "pull system" of manufacturing are found. In the push system, the production plan is divided up between the various processes, the suppliers, and the vendors, with each division creating another subordinate production schedule. These subordinate schedules are forwarded to the separate production departments. The managers in these departments dispatch the plans (that is, they schedule the manufacturing activities by taking into account delivery deadlines and the manufacturing processes) and give directions to their various manufacturing floors. The manufacturing areas make what they have been instructed to make, heedless of any other work areas, pushing the partially completed work to the next station as soon as possible.

In contrast, when a production schedule is established in the "pull system," instructions are given to the final process of the entire manufacturing sequence. When production originates at the final station, this last station uses parts that have been prepared and are waiting to be used. As the parts are used, the stock of prepared parts becomes depleted. The final process then goes to the previous process to "buy" (pull) parts from that earlier process. In some factories the workers from the downstream station do not go directly to the upstream station to pull parts, but instead go to a "store" (a coupling point between stations where there is some intermediate inventory) to "buy" (pull) parts. Because the upstream process only replaces the parts "sold" to the downstream process, it needs to make only enough parts to replenish the stock in the store. This pull manufacturing system is the theory behind the *kanban* system. In order to successfully run this *kanban* system, innovations need be made to ensure that the products flow smoothly through the factory; in other words, it is necessary to introduce JIT methods and to make improvements to the work stations.

In addition to *kanban*, there are other interesting, basic terms of the JIT vocabulary. Among these are *andon*, which designates the device used for a lighted visual signal; *hoshin*, which refers to policies, strategies, and directions; and *kaizen*, the fundamental attitudes of continuous improvement. Another often recurrent term is *mizusumashi*.

Mizusumashi literally means "whirligig beetle." The term is derived from likening the operators lithely swarming around a crowded factory to the whirligig beetles skimming around on the top of a pond. There are two application meanings to the term. One of these is two or three operators running multiple processes on a single manufacturing line. The other is in describing the operators, busily going back and forth between processes, carrying parts, ensuring that there are no defective parts getting in the way, responding to problems in the lines, and performing setup changes.

Let's trace the activities that the Fukugai Works ran between August 1986 and August 1987 as part of their implementation of JIT. Here, JIT was deployed into every workshop.

August through December, 1986

The direction of the consultants was toward the 5S's, the creation of flow lines, and the *kanban* system.

Their improvement plans included the following:

- *Building A (assembly factory):* establishing designated placement locations, using *kanban* in the door preparation process, establishing U-shaped lines in the door preparation process

- *Building PS (wooden parts processing plant):* establishing designated placement locations, creating flow manufacturing in the door finishing process, using *kanban* on the frame members
- *Building K (metal parts processing plant):* establishing designated placement locations, creating flow manufacturing in the wooden frame line process, using *kanban* on the wooden frame line

January 1987

The direction of the consultants was toward implementing the pull system, reexamining stores, and shortening changeover times.

Their improvement plans included the following:

- *Building A:* using *kanban* on the door preparation process from assembly forward
- *Building PS:* daily delivery of wash basins from Building S (sink and miscellaneous materials assembly plant)
- *Building K:* modifying the layout of the wooden frame line

February 1987

The direction of the consultants was toward performing *mizusumashi*, manufacturing daily quotas, and converting to work-top lines.

Their improvement plans included the following:

- *Building A:* the trial of the one or two lot-per-month assembly system
- *Building PS:* daily deliveries of cardboard from Building S
- *Building K:* shortening changeover times in the sink line

March 1987

The direction of the consultants was toward supplying parts sets, creating flow manufacturing systems, and reducing work-in-process inventory.

Their improvement plans included the following:

- *Building A: mizusumashi* of Line C (the Sun Shell assembly line) and Line D (the Sun Valet assembly line)
- *Building PS:* using *kanban* for the cross panels and mirror boards
- *Building K:* moving the rework process to a production line

April 1987

The direction of the consultants was toward increasing the efficiency of the lines, creating flow manufacturing lines, and three-day manufacturing.

Their improvement plans included the following:

- *Building A:* using *andon* and *kanban* on lines C and D
- *Building PS:* daily manufacture of soft forms, daily manufacture of side panels
- *Building K:* reducing finished sink inventory

May 1987

The direction of the consultants was toward mixed flow production, creating flow manufacturing lines, and three-day manufacturing.

Their improvement plans included the following:

- *Building A: mizusumashi* on all lines
- *Building PS:* using *kanban* on the doors
- *Building K:* direct shipment of long counter tops to all regions, shortening changeover times

June 1987

The direction of the consultants was toward sheet number ordered assembly, shortening changeover times, and head count reductions.

Their improvement plans included the following:

- *Building A:* mixed manufacturing in sink/counter assembly
- *Building PS:* flash line, boring line, and reducing inventory between panels
- *Building K:* direct connection to seam and ring lines

July 1987

The consultants now considered where to go with JIT from here.

Their improvement plans included the following:

- *Building A:* trials of sheet-number-ordered assembly on the door-hanging line
- *Building PS:* shortening the time to finish the top panels in Building S
- *Building K:* eliminating scrapped sinks

Summarizing the major activities of the year, we see the following:

1. *4S promotion:* Designating placement locations, clarifying quantities, eliminating the waste of searching for things.
2. *Shortening assembly lines:* If the processes are distant from each other and there are problems in a process, the preceding and subsequent processes cannot resolve them. Because the processes cannot help each other, they tend to ignore each other. Shortening the assembly lines eliminated these problems.

3. *Shortening changeover times:* In order to perform small lot, highly diversified manufacturing and parallel production, changeover times have been improved.
4. *Systemizing preparation processes:* In order to realize flow manufacturing, it is necessary to eliminate work-in-process inventory and to devote parts lines to JIT processing. This aspect cannot be done in segments because implementing JIT should follow, whenever possible, the path of process flow. Hence, rather than more comprehensive attempts, selected processes in the middle of production lines have been targeted for JIT introduction.
5. *Creating U-shaped lines:* U-shaped lines were used to promote multifunctionality and reduce the number of workers needed to run the operations.

Hirano liked to say that "improvements are results," meaning that if the improvements have no effect, then the various activities involved in the improvements are meaningless. And "S-JIT" indeed had various effects.

First, in inventory levels, using April 1983 as the index (100 percent), the inventory levels in the Fukugai Works fell to 85 percent by April 1984, to 23 percent by April 1985, to 22 percent by April 1986, and to 21 percent by 1987, a reduction to one part in five in only four years time. On the other hand, taking the inventory index in the Kiryū Works to be 100 percent in 1985, the levels were 75 percent in 1986 and 51 percent in 1987.

Second, if productivity in a particular assembly plant in the Fukugai Works is indexed to a value of 100 percent for April 1985, then productivity was 137 percent for 1986, 151 percent for 1987, and 159 percent for 1988. In another assembly plant in the Fukugai Works the values were 103 percent for 1986, 124 percent for 1987, and 149 percent for 1988. The numbers for the best comparable assembly plant in the Kiryū Works are 117 percent for 1986, 125 percent for 1987, and 132 percent for 1988.

Economizing labor (or reducing the head count) indicates the number of workers no longer needed for operations. This figure includes both direct and indirect labor rationalized. In 1987 Fukugai Works employed twenty-two fewer people than in 1986; Kiryū Works, thirty-one; and Heta Works, twenty-seven, for a total reduction in labor of eighty people.

Yoshino sums it up, "The concept of JIT was an exact fit with our shift to the development of products with high levels of added value. This perfect marriage brought excellent results even though the workshops were skeptical. One must be careful — it isn't hard to leave things as they are, taking the easy way out. Although we have completed our first companywide attempt at JIT, in the future we will integrate it with the technology already possessed by our company to develop JIT even further. This is to say, we want to take the challenge of integrating a movement to raise quality into a simultaneous promotion of JIT."

Company President Suyama added, "We won't forget the concept of JIT." When asked what that concept is, he replied, "Thorough elimination of waste — and it is important to note that 'thorough' means never regressing to how things were before JIT."

CHAPTER TWO

Even the President Did His Work Standing Up

Akita Shindengen Industries

What Is Youth?

August 9, 1988. An airplane has circled many times — the dense fog up the Omonogawa River from the Sea of Japan had socked in the Akita Airport. Touchdown had been delayed for nearly an hour. From here there would be a forty-five-minute taxi ride through the rice-growing region to the city of Honjō. Because it was coming up on the night of the Kyūbon festival honoring departed ancestors, no farm workers could be seen through the fields.

In this part of Japan whole villages customarily join together in preparation for the Kyūbon festival. They cut down weeds along the road and around their houses. Firewood prepared for the winter is neatly stacked. This, the hottest week of the year, passes quickly, the people doing nothing save receiving guests, eating, and drinking. Multicolored plants in profuse bloom are offered to the Buddha at the local shrines. The Kyūbon tradition is firmly, unchangingly entrenched with these country folk, the rituals in complete harmony with the surrounding conditions.

The taxi driver says that this year the growth of the rice is three to four days later than usual. Another week's delay will spell disaster for the farmers. The famous Festival of the Lanterns ended yesterday in the city of Akita. The taxi stops in front of a factory on the outskirts of the city of Honjō. As the door opens, one feels the excitement of seeing this factory which, in at least one aspect, is unique in the world.

In the formal entranceway, one's eye is drawn to a large wall hanging upon which a saying is written gracefully in India ink:

> *Youth is not a certain period in the life of humankind, youth is a state of mind — superior creativity, strong will, burning passions, undauntable valor, a sense of adventure when confronting difficulties. This is "youth."*

Earning the "PM Prize"

In March 1983, Taimei Takazaki was appointed president of Akita Shindengen. Entering Shindengen Industries after graduating from the humanities program in college, Takazaki served in the materials department for three years, developed a production control system as a systems engineer (SE), saw the operations of the entire company as he served in the administrative planning office, experienced marketing development as a sales engineer, and was involved in the semiconductor sales promotion. He came to Akita through a twenty-year journey. With his long history of technological positions, he never dreamed of becoming president of the manufacturing subsidiary.

Many tasks faced Takazaki, the company's fourth president. On arrival, he wondered if it was really all right that the factory operated at such a leisurely pace. For Takazaki, who had always been on the first line of management fighting exacting demands, the production factory must have seemed quite relaxed at first glance. And to one raised in the city, the area around Akita must have seemed terribly remote.

In 1983, semiconductors sold quite well. Akita was often stymied, however, by having a year's worth of back orders. Takazaki knew many things that the company must do. Beginning the following year, activity after activity was supported by the pillars of motivation and education. The work force during that time period moved from static potential to action and achievement.

The company had introduced the Modular Arrangement of Predetermined Time Standards (or MODAPTS) system in 1984. MODAPTS is a simple operations research method developed by Australian professor G. C. Heyde. When compared to previous methods, MODAPTS is simpler to master and more accurate. It can be used in a broad range of applications, including establishing and improving operations and performing diagnosis of supplier companies. MODAPTS is actively used by many companies. The entire Sony group adopted MODAPTS, as did Hitachi, Fuji Film, and others. The MODAPTS method helped enhance the quality of improvements made by those quality control (QC) circles that had fallen into stagnation.

The next project was the challenge of the major target, the "PM Prize" for preventive maintenance. Of the companies with total employee involvement in Total Productive Maintenance (TPM), a program for production maintenance, the Japan Institute of Plant Maintenance (JIPM) selects the organization with the most excellent program for the award. While TQC is a program that targets people in the company, TPM is a companywide movement that targets the optimization of equipment use. TPM is indispensable in JIT, which requires zero breakdowns and zero defects. It is currently employed by well over a hundred Japanese firms and is spreading overseas as well.

The company's TPM program, kicked off at the end of 1985, saw its final work floor inspection on August 3, 1988, and won the PM Prize.

The Complicated Semiconductor Manufacturing Process

Akita Shindengen, a wholly owned subsidiary of Akita Shindengen Industries, founded in 1945, had forecast sales to be $23 million by 1988. It employs 154 men and 232 women, totaling 386 employees, of which 76 are classified as part-time employees. The products manufactured by the company are semiconductor components, including silicon rectifiers (diodes), bidirectional two-contact thyristors, transistors, and hybrid IC's (HIC). Semiconductors are not of themselves independent products but are used as parts for composite devices.

For example, diodes have functions that make them usable in rectifying both high-voltage and electronics power sources. Thus they are used in a variety of products including microwave ovens, VCRs, hair dryers, office equipment and computers, and communications equipment. The thyristor has the combined functions of an ignition switch, of an electronic starter, and of an electronic switching device. It is used in lighters, florescent lights, emergency lights, gas equipment, and all varieties of timers. The fact that transistors in Japan are called "the rice (or staff of life) of manufacturing" comes from the range and number of applications of semiconductors.

Characteristics of semiconductor manufacturing are that: (1) the number of parts stations are few and (2) the processes are repeated many times. The manufacturing process can be divided into two parts, the front end (the chemical treatments and processes) and the back end (the labor-intensive assembly process). Even today it is difficult to rationally respond to the non-linear, convoluted manufacturing flow that is characterized by the production of a highly diversified range of products in small, medium, and large lots. The company produces approximately 300 products, with monthly production volumes ranging from as many as 5 million to as low as 20,000 to 30,000 units.

The production flow is as follows:

SILICON WAFER ➤ WAFER PROCESSING ➤ ASSEMBLY ➤ SORT ➤ MARKING THE SCRAPS ➤ SHIPPING INSPECTION ➤ PACKAGING AND SHIPPING

Current Conditions of the Unstable Inputs

Takazaki, a man who claims that he has no hobbies, has plenty of time to read. While flipping through some magazines, he saw an article describing the successes of JIT. Takazaki was intrigued, and the impressions remained for a long time.

Takazaki discovered a course taught by Hiroyuki Hirano of the JIT Management Research Center, one of the training courses offered by the Akita Technopolis beginning in 1986. He immediately had two of his middle managers sign up for the course. For the next year Takazaki sought for a way to perform JIT but because he proceeded on his own, the program came to a standstill.

In March 1987 Hirano and Gotō visited the company and performed a simple diagnosis.

> *The MODAPTS method has been taught to all employees, even part-time and temporary workers, as a tool for factory improvement. We think that TPM has caused the company employees to internalize the skill of equipment maintenance. Improvements to equipment have raised overall equipment efficiencies from 67 to 85 percent, allowing the company to secure the PM Prize and giving the employees a strong sense of confidence.*

Did JIT somehow differ from the QC circles activities, the MODAPTS method, and TPM that Takazaki had introduced three years earlier?

It was completely different. Industrial engineering (IE) as a method assumed the existing process flow and operational methods and sought to improve their efficiency. Meanwhile, JIT breaks free from the status quo in all aspects from philosophies to methods. On the other hand, because it targets "zero failures, zero defects," TPM is indispensable in furthering JIT. Its emphasis of pushing equipment to the limits of its current capabilities and of increasing production volumes as much as possible, however, proceeds from a different direction. Because JIT is impossible until some of the most fundamental philosophies of the company are changed, it had a great impact. I was shocked when such great men as Hirano and Gotō told me that our current manufacturing systems were absolutely unsatisfactory.

Sensing that there were no alternatives, Takazaki retained Gotō for regular factory visits and again faced the task of implementing JIT. The new program began by changing its name from Akita Shindengen New Production System (ANPS) to JIT Akita Shindengen (JIT/AS).

The Secret of Motivation

For the time being, goals were set to have 100 improvement activities per month, to reduce the head count by twenty employees per month (a 20 percent reduction in six months), and to reduce inventory by 50 percent. "For the time being" might be misleading. Although management engaged in earnest discussion and performed various calculations in setting the goals, there really was no choice but to choose these numbers at random. Maybe, because it is only a goal, a rough estimate is good enough. But in this action lies the secret to JIT. In a sense, it is the *motivation of the people involved* that makes JIT. Regardless of how conducive external environments and conditions are, if the people do not put their hearts into it, the objectives of just-in-time cannot be realized.

Regardless of how impossible the goal may be, if the employees are behind it, success will follow.

Various rules were derived. First, a JIT promotion project team was formed consisting of eleven members, including the company president, the board of directors' factory director, the production department manager, sub-manager level functionaries, two members of the office staff, and members of the supplier company. These people can be considered the managing staff of the JIT project. Participation of the supplier factories was included so that there would be some lateral diffusion of the movement's results.

> *In order to properly perform JIT, we changed slightly the way we looked at the division of responsibilities at different levels in companywide activities. At the time of the TPM kickoff, the circle activities, which had been based on elective participation and self-management, became compulsory companywide activities. The circles changed their names to "QP Circles" and adopted an organization, paralleling the formal work organization, which was hierarchically linked and which included all company members from the company president to factory operators.*
>
> *"Q" stood for "Quality" and "P" stood for "Productivity." The system was one wherein the company president was the responsible party in the "Top QP Circle" that managed the department and section managers. The "Middle QP Circles" were headed by section managers who took care of the sub-managers. In the "Senior QP Circles" the sub-managers would see the group managers and the work group leaders, and in the "Front QP Circles" the group managers and foremen would provide leadership and management to the general operators.*
>
> *While we were promoting both TPM and JIT, we realized that if responsibility for these programs was pressed upon all employees down to the level of the first-line employees, confusion would result and the programs would not progress. Therefore, we arranged the program so that the Top and Middle QP Circles were in charge of*

JIT. In addition, we had the Senior and Front QP Circles autonomously perform the TPM activities.

These various circles established their own *hoshin* policies, strategies, and directives and were made to perform *hoshin* management. (While this term is often referred to as "hoshin planning," President Nogawa of Komatsu says that it is better translated as "hoshin management.")

The term *front* was created by Takazaki and is used only in this company. It means "the first-line employees." This system implemented TPM just as the company was about to lose vigor. The system, which went from being a bottom-up to a top-down system, a method to provide specific motivation, was an easily digestible, masterful invention by Takazaki.

Mondays and Thursdays were designated "Improvement Days." On these days the project committee would gather in the selected work area and perform the entire improvement process in one swoop, from establishing goals to performing the improvement. Traditionally, improvements are made by designating problem areas and by having the improvement group or factory workers make the improvement, with the project committee returning on a later date to view the results. The procedure here, however, was different. Except for the most major improvements, they were generally performed on the spot. At the beginning there would sometimes be a lack of focus, causing the improvement process to take time. The improvement sessions would start at three o'clock in the afternoon and last until at least ten or eleven o'clock at night. When improvements didn't go well, they were redone, and redone again.

The themes adopted were the 5S's (*seiri, seiton, seiketsu, seisō, shitsuke*) and the creation of flow manufacturing lines. Improved multifunctionality, standing operations (that is, performing work operations while standing up rather than sitting), one-piece lots, simultaneous manufacturing, and the promotion of multistation work were adopted as challenge themes to improve flow manufacturing.

The President Gets to Work

In August 1987, while JIT was gradually gaining momentum, President Takazaki suddenly started to do all of his work standing up. It wasn't just the people in the administrative office who were surprised by this — within a day, all 400 members of the company had heard about the president's strange behavior.

Since the beginning of the JIT movement, Takazaki had told himself that someday he would start to do all of his work standing up. "I heard from Mr. Gotō that if we all did our work standing up, productivity would increase 20 percent. I thought that if I expected the operators to work standing up, then I would, too. My colleagues were enthusiastic, and when I started so did they.

The workers in the production management office were the first to stand. Then the women who sorted the diodes quit sitting and instead did their work standing. Next, the workers in the assembly process before diode sorting stated that they, too, wanted to stand.

As Takazaki went through the factory in his daily routine, the time finally came. Although a couch remained in the company president's office — it would be taking it too far to ask visitors to stand — Takazaki expedited the work order for tables and desks to be constructed for "standing operations." Simulations were run to see what size and height desks were the easiest to work with.

After that, the movement spread swiftly as people wanted to stand as they did their jobs. The labor union offered no opposition. There was, however, other resistance. In the first area where people started to do their work standing up — the diode sorting station — productivity fell by 20 percent as soon as the workers started to stand. The workers weren't used to standing all day and soon became fatigued.

"When I went into the factory after five o'clock, there wasn't a soul working overtime. When I asked why, I was told that they were so tired that they couldn't work, so they went home. At break times the workers would plop right down and sit on the floor."

It wasn't just the factory workers who were tired. President Takazaki, even though only forty-eight years old, was also affected. Without telling anyone, Takazaki, his back hurting, purchased a corset-like back brace. "The younger fellows are strong, so they are probably all right, but I think that it was as hard on the temporary employees and the part-timers as it was on me!"

Takazaki began to waiver. "When I looked at the factory, I got the impression that were it not that I did my work standing up, they would have given up on the idea. If I hadn't been standing myself, I probably would have told them to all sit down."

But after two or three weeks, incredibly, the pain in Takazaki's back disappeared.

The Effectiveness of Standing Operations

The JIT consultants explained the effects of standing operations in terms of both experience and logic. Although for decades the employees in the Toyota companies have been standing as they work, there have never been any problems. When workers stand, the operations develop a rhythm, with one movement melding into the next. When operators stand, the amount of work they can do increases — operations in situations such as multifunctional U-shaped lines cannot be performed by seated workers. As tangible benefits, productivity rises more than 20 percent and space is opened up for other purposes, such as break rooms. Although difficult for workers at first, as they grow accustomed to it, working while standing becomes more pleasant than working while sitting.

As Akita Shindengen instituted standing operations, they considered keeping chairs in the plant while the standing operations were in progress, adjusting tables to the heights of the users, and so forth. During morning meetings the purpose of the standing operations was explained over and over. The company made special break rooms and provided shoes with thick, soft soles. At first, the workers made their own bamboo foot massagers because their feet hurt. After the first month, however, these also disappeared.

The result was that employees in all the workshops stood throughout the entire month of August — as did people in the general affairs, design, production engineering, accounting, and the data processing departments. Some jobs, however, just couldn't be done standing up, such as operating presses designed to be operated from a sitting position and computer keyboard work. Pregnant women and people in poor health were also not expected to stand.

As for the effects of the first year of the standing operations, Takazaki remarked, "Because we were implementing other improvements at the same time, no quantitative statistic can tell us the improvement percentage that resulted from standing operations. Speaking from my own experience, however, when I drop myself into a chair, I find it disturbing to get up each time I need to file a paper. It is more convenient to stand."

Toshiro Saito from the factory manager's JIT office remarked, "A lot of work in the assembly operations required people to stand and then sit and then stand again. But in order to have operators run multiple processes, they had to stand all the time."

Yūichi Sugaware, from the same office, emphasized the effects of the companywide movement. "I think that the biggest thing was that the company president himself was standing. A year ago we felt a sense of danger — with the rising power of the yen a portion of our work had been taken by our sister company in the Philippines. If only people on the manufacturing floors had to work standing up, there would have been complaints. Because management and indirect departments also worked standing up, however, there was a sense of camaraderie."

JIT consultant Gotō was also surprised. He had seen many cases where once a company had encountered problems with standing, it wouldn't continue. There are two ways to introduce the concept of working while standing up. One is to start small and gradually increase the number of standing operations; the other is to have everybody begin standing at the same time. This company had everyone stand together — even the president.

When asked if Akita's Tokyo division also worked standing up, Takazaki replied, "That would probably be impossible. Although our parent company is also introducing JIT, I doubt that they would stand right away. Here we have the Akita environment and the Akita culture. It is important that labor/management relations go well."

The company slowly began to recover the work that had been lost to the Philippines. Since the introduction of just-in-time, they were now able to produce less expensively.

From Batch Processing to One-Piece Processing

When one asks if the other aspects of JIT went smoothly because the company performed the most difficult part of JIT first, the answer is "No." The bottleneck in the company's JIT activities revolved around how to convert the $1.25 million batch-processing equipment to flow manufacturing. Implementation was incorporated in the following sequence.

Beginning in July, the main theme centered on flow-style production. The creation of miniproduction lines and the exposure of areas needing improvement were promoted. The main theme for August was the same, with sub-themes of not collecting all products in one place for shipping inspections and of eliminating paperwork.

September's theme was to reduce waste through combinations — attention was paid to improvements that would join the miniproduction lines to each other. Once the diodes had been assembled, the company had been sending them to an outside contractor who used a large-scale automated scrubber on the assembled parts. By developing a small-scale manual scrubber instead, the company was able to eliminate transport time and link the process directly to the subsequent molding process.

Integrated-flow production was adopted as October's theme. The goal was to make one large production line by combining the small production lines and to eliminate any of the "isolated islands" that were not part of any line at all. Moreover, a production control board was constructed as part of "visual control," standardized operations were established, and seminars on cycle time were held.

November. A model line was selected with the intent of making a large-scale production line. Improvements were made to the production control system and through the use of *kanban* a move was made toward make-to-order manufacturing through line leveling in the high-pressure diode process. This system was based on order information, subtracting the number of days needed to process the products from the day that the products must be delivered, performing a leveling strategy that pushes forward, with each station given a quota to produce only enough for the next day.

December's theme concentrated on (1) discovering areas in the overall line that needed improvements and (2) then making those improvements by attempting to create a one-piece lot system and (3) attempting to improve the equipment through linking the lines. How to reduce the lot sizes in wafer processing, how to deal with exceptions to operations, how to create a "first-in, first-out" system, cycle times (that is, in how many minutes and seconds must the work on each unit be completed), and so forth were all topics of interest.

January 1988 saw the beginning of mixed manufacturing — running many types of products on the same production line. In February, the 5S's, standard operations, and flow manufacturing were the main themes. Standardized work procedures were displayed in each work area, showing the optimal work methods and ensuring thorough standardization.

March saw efforts to laterally diffuse the successes of the model line to other work areas. The people who were no longer needed because of the increased efficiency of the model line were used in other production lines. An example of improvements diffused laterally is that both the conversion of batch processing systems in the assembly shops to one-piece processing and the move from seated working to standing work were both applied to assembly processes in the vendor factories. This month placement methods were also reexamined, clearly labeling the storage locations of all of the goods within the company. Signs were added to every storage location, showing the names of products, the names of the parts being stored, the maximum allowable number of units, the name of the preceding process, the name of the subsequent process, the name of the responsible party, and the area number. The main improvements in this instance were that maximum storage capacities were established and monthly discrepancies were visible with just a glance.

April. This month saw the promotion of "production leveling" that took into consideration types of products, production volumes, and production timing. It also saw the concentration of personnel, a trial run of the *kanban* system, and serious consideration of *mizusumashi*, at least for those personnel who are in charge of supplying parts so that there would be no parts missing from assembly kits.

The Fundamentals of Introducing New Equipment

Improving operations, equipment, and processes are necessary in the JIT process of improvement. JIT, which was basically established on inexpensive, inelegant, dirt-under-the-fingernails improvements, had added to the skills in equipment development and maintenance that had been refined through TPM. In Akita Shindengen the time had come to establish a fundamental policy (*hoshin*) pertaining to the introduction of new equipment. Takazaki was resolved not to repeat his mistake of introducing equipment using the "big boat, big guns" concept (that is, the concept that the more powerful the equipment, the better). In fact, the further the JIT program progressed, the more the giant equipment (which had cost $1.25 million) was becoming an obstruction instead of a benefit, a bottleneck in the improvement activities. Because "equipment introduction guidelines" are vital enough to be called the essence of JIT management, the following aphorisms were developed about overly optimistic equipment investment.

1. Equipment should be profitable at the production volumes given it. Equipment that needs to produce millions of units in order to be profitable will be perpetually unprofitable, because once the production

level slightly exceeds the necessary volume, the purchase of another monster machine will be necessary,
and this new machine will not be profitable until it
approaches full utilization.

Strategy for Resolution: Do not be overly optimistic in
making trial calculations. Use the numbers obtained
from the calculations wisely, so that equipment will be
profitable from the start.

2. Equipment should not process batches, but instead
continuously processes single units.

Strategy for Resolution: Small-footprint, low-cost equipment is best. Pitch time (the length of time it takes the
equipment to process one unit) should be modifiable
according to cycle time (the length of time in which one
unit must be produced).

3. Equipment should be flexible.

Strategy for Resolution: Choose equipment that is adapt-
able to the production of many types of products, and
dedicate the equipment to the line. Jigs and such
should be able to be changed between products with
ease (one touch) and with speed.

4. Equipment should have self-inspection devices such as
sensors and counters.

Strategy for Resolution: Promote what Toyota calls
"autonomation" or "automation with a human touch."
In other words, improve equipment so that they stop
themselves when they produce defects.

5. Equipment should be easy to operate and easy to
maintain.

Strategy for Resolution: Equipment that is easy to clean
and easy to oil; allows quick changeovers; has few
parts that can become worn; has easily replaceable

parts; has standardized screws that are few in number; has organized blueprints, operating manuals, and maintenance manuals; and is energy efficient, relatively quiet, and does not pollute the air or the water.

6. Equipment should be movable.
   Strategy for Resolution: Machines are equipped with casters, flexible pipes, and flexible wiring. There are no fixed conveyer lines.

7. Equipment should be self-cleaning.
   Strategy for Resolution: Equipment disposes of its own dust, trash, turnings, and so on.

8. Equipment should allow operators to stand.
   Strategy for Resolution: Equipment that is at the appropriate height to allow for operation while standing up, moves the articles being processed from left to right, and requires as few steps as possible when used in a production line.

9. Equipment should count both the number of items processed and the number of defects.

10. Equipment processing speed should work within the forecast cycle times.
    Strategy for Resolution: The higher the machining processing speed, the more stoppages there will be so that it doesn't operate faster than the lines, the more the equipment tends to break down, and the higher the equipment cost. If the equipment speed is in line with the cycle time, then even low-speed equipment is acceptable. The need for equipment stoppages should be avoided — stopping and restarting equipment ties up workers.

11. Plan equipment in context with the line.

These eleven items make up the fundamental strategy of equipment procurement learned through TPM and JIT.

An additional characteristic of the equipment improvement activities at Akita Shindengen is that the company performed improvements that were as inexpensive as possible.

For example, although the drying furnace had been set apart from the other batch processing equipment, when the direction came that all equipment was to be lined up in the logical processing sequence, the workers discovered that toaster ovens could be used for the drying process. The process that previously had taken an hour was shortened to five minutes, and the process that had treated 700-unit lots was replaced by a process with one-piece lots. Promoting the in-line concept, the company developed small washers that could be inserted into the processes. All types of economical innovations in improvements were incorporated, such as using standard store-bought flashlights as *andon* lights to inform managers when problems arose.

New Goals

So what were the results of the one-year whirlwind implementation of JIT? Although the objective was to reduce the head count by 119 people in six months, by December 1987 the company had achieved a reduction of 123 people. In 1988, between January and March the head count was reduced by another 23 people. The number of improvement projects, 240 at the six-month point, saw a large-scale increase to 493 by the seventh month, 802 by the ninth month, 1,071 by the eleventh month, and 1,210 by the twelfth month. As for the inventory index, if set at 100 at the start of the JIT program in June 1987, the index fell to 91 by October, to 88 by December, and to 84 by January 1988. It reached 76 by April 1988.

Takazaki was not fully satisfied by these numbers. "One year has passed and we have finally reached the stage where the equipment is arranged according to the process order of the various products, and where we are on the verge of full establishment of small lot manufacturing. In the true meaning of flow manufacturing-based JIT, we have only just begun."

Takazaki already had a new set of goals he had started to put into effect. He showed a pervasive confidence that the company could accomplish the following:

- establish thorough flow operations and make improvements based on standardized operations planned in detail down to the second
- expand the *kanban*-based pull production system
- incorporate such systems as *poka-yoke* (or mistake-proofing) into the flow manufacturing

JIT's Starting Point

Takazaki was able to open the box of JIT magic and take a look inside. For him, the world was completely different once the box was opened. Lately he has been speaking to other managers, but finds little sympathy because they can't understand the spell and enchantment of JIT.

In contrast to most managers, Takazaki didn't start out as an engineer. Had Takazaki come from a technical background, he probably would have had one or two strategies to implement as soon as he became the new president. With his humanities background, however, he did not compete on the basis of technology but instead addressed the "people" issues of management and control.

As a novice at manufacturing, he saw and heard everything with new eyes and was able to accept it obsequiously. This was fortunate for the introduction of JIT. A company president from an engineering office might have been unable to lead his company in a production revolution.

When one looks closely, because Takazaki's sights were set on people, he created devices to develop people. The wall hanging mentioned at the beginning of this chapter, "What is youth," was one such device. Since Takazaki came to the company, a company song has been written. Company employees wrote the words and Takazaki composed the music. These devices provided the arena for just-in-time because JIT is a revolution in awareness. Regardless of how many JIT "techniques" are put to use, if the level of awareness regresses, the program cannot progress. Conversely, if the company strides forward with true JIT awareness, effects will be seen regardless of the number of techniques applied.

CHAPTER THREE

Interaction Between the Customer and the Factory Floor

Matsushita Electrical Works, Ltd., Relay Administrative Office

A Box of Candy in Return

The JIT Workshop Improvement Report Conference began at one o'clock in the afternoon on June 20th in the Ise factory conference room. The meeting included spectators from other companies and presenters from affiliate companies. The presenters were of production floor section head, floor chief, and sub-manager level.

These were report conferences held every six months since the factory instituted just-in-time in which the results of JIT activities were reported and evaluated by the administration. Supplier companies also participated. The report conferences were significant, and the administrative vice president was always in attendance.

Michiko Murakami from Manufacturing Section 3 reported the successes her group had with "U-line conversion of relay production." Then, she announced to everyone that the improvements mentioned were done entirely by female employees. "Although sometimes when we worked late at night to make the improvements, we asked ourselves, `Why are we doing this?' We eventually managed to switch over to the type of equipment we had hoped for."

After reporting the successes of the U-shaped line, she got a chuckle by saying, "We used two characteristics unique to women — those of being both sensitive and tenacious — to eventually achieve our goals. So in the future, we won't overly concern ourselves with what the men are doing, confident that we will be able to greatly increase productivity elsewhere."

She concluded by saying, "While we are not satisfied with these results, others have been. Recently somebody from one of the sales locations came to the factory, brought us a box of candy, and told us that the shortened lead times were truly helpful to salespeople. At that time our joy wasn't because of the candy, but because of what he had said to us."

The words of the tiny woman who made the presentation represented the women who comprised 80 percent of the work force in the factory and echoed as a portent of Matsushita Electrical Work's production revolution.

For the User

First of all, speed. This year the company is nearing its seventieth year since its foundation. However, the past years hang on the next five or ten years — we will soon be washed over by a wave of change far greater than any we have navigated in the past. We have no choice but to progress from this point forth. Because of this, the slogan "Amenity and Intelligence" (or A&I) (meaning to scientifically address issues such as comfort) has been adopted as our company's corporate identity.

In its ultimate form, the target of our work and of our products is to provide optimal pleasure to the users. If we keep this goal in mind, then haste in the process will not be a problem. On the other hand, goals such as these are painful to those who are behind in their skills.

So said Toshio Miyoshi soon after he was appointed president of the company in January 1988.

Matsushita Electrical Work's monthly sale calls average $178. With 147,000 different product items tracked by its computer, each product item averages $3,260 per month. The company has 200,000 sales outlets. The company ranks twenty-ninth in sales among Japanese manufacturers, with a reported income ranking of twentieth. There are 14,168 employees, 2,300 of whom are in management. As of November 1987 the average age of the employees is 34.6 years. The company has fourteen factories and fifty-five sales bases in Japan and five factories and thirteen sales bases overseas. These statistics indicate that Matsushita Electrical Works is a typical Japanese "super company."

Once the organization was set up, inconsistencies began to appear. Moreover, the organization was intractable with a strong instinct for self-preservation. It is President Miyoshi's belief that because an organization is made up of people, if individual members don't continually carry the torch of progressing tomorrow beyond the level of today, then one day, unavoidably, the company will falter. Therefore, he believes that nothing is more important in his role as company president than to thoroughly promote A&I. "And the starting point," he says, "is the customer."

Seventy Years Old

Matsushita Electrical Works became independent of Matsushita Electric Industrial Company in 1946 under the direction of the wartime general headquarters. Since its break from the other company, business has centered on the production of wiring accessories, synthetic resin products, and conduit pipes. After that, the company procured from the United States the technology pertaining to laminated base plates, entered into plastic construction materials, and expanded its system to include 3,000 electrical stores. Progressive strategies in manufacturing and marketing were both effective and smooth.

Currently, twenty-three divisions include thirteen electrical equipment divisions, five residential divisions, three electronic materials divisions, and two control equipment divisions. In fiscal year 1987 the electrical equipment divisions accounted for 57.2 percent of total sales, the residential divisions accounted for 26.3 percent, the electronic materials divisions accounted for 9.9 percent, the control equipment divisions accounted for 6.5 percent, with other sales making up 0.1 percent. Exports accounted for 6.5 percent of sales. Intelligent wiring systems, the *tsukerun* automated pickling machine, and a shower are in new product development. The various divisions each have their own unique products, including bath units, thermal regeneration electrically heated floor panels, large-scale fluorescent light displays, and home elevators. President Miyoshi adds:

I believe that Matsushita Electrical Works is probably the only company in the world that engages in such a large-scale and complex line of integrated products pertaining to electrical work, construction of electrical equipment, residential construction materials, and all types of residential construction equipment.

Despite that belief, the company does not yet have the ability to respond to all of the systemization and moves to intelligent systems typified by home automation (HA). Along with strengthening the company's niche technologies and engineering technologies and developing the marketing project team system, my dream is to see the company raise the level of its A&I to world class levels by assertively expanding its domestic and foreign cooperation in off-shore manufacturing and by developing bold merger and acquisition activities.

Also internal appeal cannot be overlooked. It is necessary to add speed to the corporate power that is based on emphasizing "real products in real work sites," an emphasis developed over the past seventy years. Speed alone, however, is worthless. Without a strategy, the company image will not improve. And because top management's strategy is paramount, the strategies of the chief administrative officers and of the division managers must be made clear.

Monopolistic Markets and Markets with Excessive Competition

Assistant Director Masayuki Himeda of the JIT office relates the following overview of the Ise factory.

In 1971 the Ise factory split off from the Tsuu factory to become a dedicated control equipment and automation parts factory. The factory in the city of Tsuu in the Mie Prefecture carries on the manufacture of the wiring accessories produced by the venerated Konosuke Matsushita at the time of the company's founding. And of all of the sites in the Matsushita corporation, this factory is regarded as having a great deal of tradition. It is an integrated wiring accessories manufacturing plant with main products including wiring accessories for residential construction, equipment construction, and household use. Its products also include information, fire alarm, burglar alarm, signal, and accident prevention systems and other microswitches and connectors. The company can boast that its wiring accessories are in the top market position, with over 80 percent market share. Even the large-scale integrated equipment makers use various plug sockets and switches made in this factory. With strong production technology and equipment superiority, the factory employs 1,500 people and produces 6,000 different products.

Then there is the Ise factory. The factory is a dedicated manufacturer of relays and takes the products through design, fabrication, and assembly. However, unlike the market for the wiring accessories of the Tsuu factory, the market for relays is fiercely competitive. The factory employs about 850 people, of which about 80 percent are young women who work in assembly operations.

The relationship between the Tsuu and Ise factories is that parts are fabricated in Tsuu and assembled in Ise. Both factories report to the control equipment division.

Himeda said, "The reason why the Ise factory was made independent of the Tsuu factory is that we thought that there would be a shortage of assembly personnel in the future. At any rate, Ise is a peaceful site. There is no other place like this — within the factory compound there are ten-odd ancient burial mounds." In the spring, rows of cherry trees bloom profusely, and in the fall, the *matsutake* mushrooms can be picked on the grounds — the factory is a unique Japanese factory, surrounded with greenery. The large, 18,000-square meter compound houses two administrative buildings and five production facilities.

An Integrated Production/Management System

First of all, embarking on Matsushita Electrical Works' Ise factory JIT program (or MI/JIT) began with the resolution to establish an integrated production control system worthy of this information age.

From Akira Ishizawa, manager of the relay department, I heard the circumstances causing the factory to attempt MI/JIT.

"Japanese relays are ahead of the crowd in terms of their high quality levels, lead times, cost, and reliability. Half of this product is earmarked for export. However, when we were hit with a rapidly rising yen two years ago, we started a companywide activity to combine production and management."

This companywide activity was to implement the integrated production and control system called WINNER, an acronym for "World Information Network and New Production" system.

"Although business in control products was going full-sail with a tail wind," Ishizawa said, "we experienced great difficulty when the business was destabilized by the severe rise in the value of the yen. To sail these stormy seas, we couldn't just rely on the *kamikaze*, the holy winds of the gods that blow to ensure Japanese triumphs. Rather, we knew that the winning edge would be achieved by returning to the basics of the Matsushita spirit and creating a corporate culture that could satisfy the diversified customer."

There was nothing unusual about this strategy to ensure continuing and overwhelming market superiority by differentiating quality, cost, and delivery lead times.

To accomplish this goal, the WINNER-integrated production and control system was proposed in a two-pronged attack to reform lead times. The attack included (1) the formation of an integrated production control system, a total information system, and (2) the full establishment of new production methods, a wholesale reduction in manufacturing lead times.

Prior to becoming the manager of the relay division, Ishizawa had already been thinking about creating a production control system using computers. However, because the division was now pushed to the wall by the rising yen and by the need to shorten lead times, thinking was not enough. Action was required.

Once a product inquiry is received, it moves from product flow to production flow to goods flow — the three major factors that determine delivery lead times. First, a distinction is made between the flow of products into the sales department and the flow of goods from the factory to the customer. Computers already process 70 to 80 percent of the information from the sale locations and sales representatives (the product flow nodes) scattered across the country. The problem to be solved by the new system was tracking the production flow and goods flow in the factory.

Ishizawa taught that the full establishment of an information system that could respond efficiently to changes in market demand and the key to making such a system was to create a make-to-order production system through a large-scale reduction of manufacturing lead times.

Takeshi Terahara, the assistant manager of the relay department, was appointed the head of the new "Production Flow Project" and began to make drastic cuts. Large projects do not advance through hesitation. Nothing ever gets started without people like Terahara, people who talk straight and are not afraid to be disliked a little by others. The analyses of the project team had this sort of directness.

Two separate channels are used by the company in marketing relays. One of these is the "manufacturing equipment products channel." Using this channel, products must always be physically present in the sales locations or else they will not sell. The other channel is the "public products channel." In this channel the relay department delivers directly to the customers. It was decided that the inventory levels in the first channel were to be reduced as much as possible; in the second channel, the lead times were to be reduced in a single motion from one week to two or three days.

The structure and objectives of the WINNER program had been decided. But when the project team got together with a particular computer manufacturer to plan the computer system, they ran into a major barrier. Sighing, Terahara related the following:

*In the past twenty years, several dozen circular letters pertaining
to computerization have come back vetoed. It's enough to discourage
someone. We haven't done very well. The capabilities of the hardware have certainly progressed. And recently software has progressed as well. If the manufacturing floor hasn't the ability to
assimilate technology, however, the technology is useless regardless
of how many computers the company buys. Moreover, even without
computers, if the factory is being run correctly, it will be able to produce the products.*

*The computer is a weapon and there should be effects as soon as
it is put to use. If you ask what conditions there must be in the factory in order to have these effects, the answer is "simple is best."
The systems in the factory must be simple. When computers and the
factory floor mesh with each other — in other words, when computers and the factory work in harmony like two gears — then it
becomes possible to make products that truly respond to the market.*

The first time that Terahara and the consultant Takeshi
Takahashi met they had an earnest discussion about computers. Although Takahashi is not with JIT Research, he previously developed production control software for a large
computer software house. Together they began to work on
the challenge of Matsushita Electrical Works' JIT program, a
program targeting world class enterprise.

The circumstances in the factory changed dramatically.
The factory improvements became preliminary skirmishes in
the struggle to create the JIT system. Himeda was from the
MI/JIT office and thus not officially part of the Ise factory
organization. Instead he was part of the computer room,
which was part of the systems section that reported directly
to the operations department. While he remained in that position, he also accepted the responsibility to promote factory
improvements.

Himeda had thought to first start a model JIT program at
the Tsuu factory and then take it to the Ise factory. In this

process, a particular man surfaced as a key player — the relay manufacturing department manager, Rikiō Takeuchi. Takeuchi played a central role in bringing computers in as an experiment — with effects far beyond expectations.

"The reason for our success? It's enthusiasm. The people on the assembly factory floor worked with great tenacity," said Ishizawa, his eyes narrowing with pleasure.

"It was said that if Takahashi looked at the factory, production would immediately double. This was a shock to us — over the thirty years that we have been in manufacturing we have developed a pride in our work. At first we thought that the idea of doubling production just by lining up the processes in process sequence was overly optimistic," said Takeuchi. After a pause he added with apparent pleasure, "But the effects are approaching that point now."

The JIT program is on the verge of expanding to the control equipment division and the affiliated companies.

Looking Back

Even companies such as Matsushita Electrical Works occasionally experience misunderstandings. These misunderstandings sometimes are tied to fundamental mistakes. Ishizawa quietly related the following story.

Until he became division manager two years earlier, Ishizawa had been in charge of production engineering at the Tsuu factory. He performed development activities to optimize the precision of the dies in the processes, to bring the press processes to their optimal speeds, and so forth. For thirty years he had skillfully sought to improve the manufacture of machine components.

On the other hand, for years it was the belief that in assembly operations, if the parts are only machined correctly, anyone could put them together. While this is true for the assembly of wiring accessories, which involves assembling large volumes of only a few product types, it is not true for the assembly of relays, where 70 percent of the products are special orders.

In the case of wiring accessories, each product type has a total monthly production of one or two million units. But the highest running relay has only a volume of about 100,000 units per month, and most relays only run 10,000 or 1,000 units per month. There was a temporary "relay boom" after the oil shock, when the company responded to the market need by expanding equipment. "After the boom ended, and the yen finally increased in power, we wondered what it was that we had been doing right until then."

Matsushita's management belief in "one type of industry, one type of work" was strong. Because the divisions were to make a profit, and because all authority and responsibility rested on their shoulders, the division managers could not do whatever they felt like — if their divisions were not profitable, they would lose their jobs.

Once the relay boom was over and the value of the yen rose, the relay division fell to be the least esteemed division in the company.

"It wasn't just the fault of production engineering. In the old days there was a distinct division — 'I'm the guy who makes the equipment and you are the guy who uses it.'" Without really understanding the needs of the workshop, equipment and production engineering were apt to push for high-level automation and precision.

"The people in manufacturing listed all of the obstructions to their operations: 'The parts aren't made with enough precision,' 'the machines are no good,' 'the product designs are flawed,' and so forth."

There is also the fundamental belief that in the factory, if the workers are doing what they are told to do, everything is fine. When there are defects, people make excuses that naturally the parts or the equipment are bad.

"Although at first there were various complaints, we tried to use the equipment in operations ourselves. Once we started to make improvements to the equipment, the complaints disappeared."

During the introduction of JIT, the maps of the Tsuu factory parts processes and of the Tsuu factory assembly processes changed. Based on Takahashi's counsel that the division should pay more attention to production flows in manufacturing, the production processes from the Tsuu factory were transferred one after another to Ise.

"Just when I thought we were going to have to build another production facility to house the new processes, factory improvements freed up enough space so that the need for the new building was obviated. Usually the workers make a fuss that they don't have enough room, and managers are constantly telling them to be tolerant. But just the opposite has happened — the factory workers are saying that they don't need another building," laughed Takeuchi.

Jobs Should Be Easy

Today the Ise factory is Matsushita Electrical Works' leading factory in JIT promotion. JIT factory improvement is henceforth part of the curriculum of study of all section managers throughout the company organization. Three factories in the company have implemented JIT, including the Tatsuno Matsushita factory and the Obihiro Matsushita factory; some of the affiliated subsidiary companies even show the impetus to surpass the parent company.

"A major factor is that we are on the verge of establishing a mood that no longer ignores the 'dirt-under-the-fingernails' part of the factory when trying to raise efficiency," said Terahara when evaluating how much the empty space was increasing as the production lines became tighter through improvement activities.

However, the more the program gets up to speed, the more problems there are associated with it.

"JIT is a production revolution," said Terahara, "but this should not mean that the work force is forced to work harder or abused in other ways. Actually, jobs should become easier."

What did Terahara mean when he said that "jobs should become easier?" The answer is found in the following words of Konosuke Matsushita, the founder of this great company.

> *The appearance of a worker with perspiration on his forehead is priceless, but perpetually working so that one constantly perspires is not wise. It is equal to the sight of a man who, instead of taking the train, trudges along the path between the stations on the Tokaido Line as in the old days. The fifty-three post stations of the Tokaido Line are making progress, from walking to palanquin, from palanquin to train, from train to airplane — and, as the days pass, the amount of perspiration on the forehead of the man decreases. Isn't it in this that we see the course of progress in human life?*
>
> *Working more than a man's share in an hour's time is a priceless effort; however, the ability to work less than an hour with even greater results is also valuable. Isn't it in this that the progress of the work methods of man is seen? Creativity is imperative, for although work is valuable, innovation and creativity in that work is desirable. The forehead covered with perspiration is commendable, but we should also praise the perspiration-free, relaxed forehead.*
>
> *This is not being lazy. This is an exhortation to innovate to make jobs easier. I want you to work together to innovate ways to work with ease and to work with excellent results. Out of this will be born prosperity for all society. (From "One Day, One Talk," October 1952.)*

The human resources department has taken the initiative to hold labor/management JIT implementation conferences. The implementation of JIT gives rise to many topics pertaining to labor/management relations that must be resolved in conference; topics such as cross-training, multifunctionality, standing operations, modifications to job descriptions, reexaminations of compensation systems, and so forth. These topics include wages after the skills levels of the workers improve through cross-training and multifunctionality (running multiple processes) and after determining how much of an extra load is, or is not, put on the workers when work is performed standing up. The company's point of view must be manifest in advance, and there needs to be an agreement about standing operations.

Companies of all sizes have already implemented JIT. There is at this time, however, no report of other companies that hold discussions with the union in advance about intensification of labor and modifications to job descriptions. For instance, because (from an efficiency standpoint), standing operations is a JIT method that is especially essential, the implementers want to use this tool at all costs. Historically, however, there is resistance from the operators.

In contrast, when standing operations was implemented in this factory, the need for the change and its rationality were established in advance. Operating parameters were explained in detail, including allowing the workers to decide whether or not to participate in the program of standing and modifications of the operating environment — which included the construction of a break room. Added to this was some degree of freedom in choosing shifts, operations, and break times. In these areas as well, it can be seen that Matsushita Electrical Works' handling of JIT was far from ordinary.

Workshop Improvement Report Conference

The "MI/JIT Workshop Improvement Report Conference" presented findings from seven workshops and nine theme presentations. The list included here is followed with more detailed explanations.

1. Improving productivity through standardized operations
2. Making a U-shaped line
   Adapting to increased production
   Improving profitability through flow manufacturing of relays
3. Improvements of processes on a highly diversified, small lot production line
4. Improved lead time
5. Improving the processes in machining the relay terminal blocks
6. Developing relay U-shaped lines and the WINNER program
7. Improving productivity through flow manufacturing of relays

Improving Productivity Through Standardized Operations

The relay manufacturing department, Manufacturing Section 1, began a one-year project, from June 1987 to May 1988. Activities were aimed at three points:

- introducing JIT and adapting to increased production levels
- gaining full participation in the 5S's
- reducing waste and standardizing operations

The plan of action for Stage 1 of JIT, from June through November 1987, would involve:

1. arranging the equipment in the order of the process flow
2. connecting manual operations (having the operators run multiple processes)
3. freeing employees for other work
4. connecting equipment (having the operators run multiple processes)
5. reducing temporary stoppages and performing the red tag strategy
6. reducing wasted motion

Stage 2 of JIT, from December 1987 through March 1988, would continue with:

1. reducing handling operations
2. addressing process defect issues
3. yellow line indicators (for routing shop floor traffic), *kanban, andon*
4. reducing the waste of on-hand inventory
5. improving changeovers
6. improving display standardization
7. work-in-process *kanban* and visual control

The objectives were threefold: reducing work-in-process inventory, improving productivity, and economizing labor. Listed here are some examples of actual improvements.

The creation and display of a product changeover checklist. Before the improvements, when it came time to changeover between products, the changeover was done relying on the memories of the experienced operators. When the work had to be done by anyone else, memos were used to communicate the procedures. Consequently, there were mistakes, a low awareness of abnormalities and problems, and times when defects were produced without anyone noticing. Obviously, special care was required in running the processes.

In response to this situation, the important parts of the changeover processes were put into a simple checklist that was displayed near the operators, resulting in smooth changeovers and a reduction in mistakes.

Reducing changeover times between products in the tooling and soldering lines. Because the equipment changeover for the new product lot could not begin until the previous lot had gone through the soldering process, the automated tooling line had to be stopped while soldering was being done. Through (1) redistributing the responsibilities for performing the changeovers and (2) introducing parallel operations, the monthly changeover times between products was reduced from nine hours to four hours, more than a 50 percent reduction.

The results of incorporating these and various other improvements was that within the year productivity rose to 140 percent, 25 percent of the work-in-process inventory was eliminated, and the head count was reduced by fifteen workers.

Process improvements in machining the relay terminal blocks. The Obihiro Matsushita Works had a young motivated work force. Their enthusiasm for JIT overwhelmed even the parent company.

This factory is developing a JIT program called JITOM (*JIT in the Obihiro Matsushita Works*). Headquartered in the production engineering section, program promoters have adopted the slogan, "Trace causes to their ends and eliminate losses," in their approach to the following themes:

* Thoroughly eliminate waste and implement one-touch die exchange.
* Decrease lot sizes, double the number of product

changeovers, and reduce inventory.

The process flow in the machining of the relay terminal block goes from the metal-trimming press process to the simultaneous plastic formation process to the terminal block process to the assembly process.

The improvement targets were aimed to:

- adapt to highly diversified, small lot manufacturing through implementing one-touch changeovers
- perform a next-process pull system by using *kanban*

The improvement goals were:

- to reduce changeover times to under ten minutes
- to raise the number of changeovers to sixty
- to reduce work-in-process inventory to 60,000 units
- to shorten the lead time to one day

The following areas were examined:

- Can die changes be done without stopping the entire line?
- Can they be done without using tools?
- Can it be done by one worker in ten minutes?

Improvements were made in the following individual operations:

- heat fusion process — implementing horizontal-push exchange clamps and eliminating the need for adjustments
- contact-point caulking process — eliminating the need to adjust the insertion of the contact points and eliminating the need for the exchange of adsorption pins
- setting up other die stand-by platforms and eliminating tools and jigs

After one year, the following results were achieved:
- Die changeovers that had taken 270 minutes were shortened to 6 minutes 45 seconds.
- The changeover frequency was 47; the target was 60. (If the next process requires 60, the goal will be reached.)
- The work-in-process inventory achieved was 45,000 units (surpassing the goal).
- One-day lead times were achieved.

Once the presentations had all been completed, the consultant Takahashi, who had been asked to provide criticism and review, was surprisingly harsh in his evaluation. He indicated the following items as major topics for discussion:

1. There needs to be the awareness that JIT is not simply a method for rationalizing the production process. JIT reflects productivity, quality, cost, and delivery lead times into sales, product development, cost structures, and the market.
2. A sluggish work floor attitude must be eliminated. Go into the work areas and ask people if they really want to work there. It is the responsibility of floor managers to help workers value their work. Safety falls into the domain of the engineers.
3. Make the equipment half its current size and weight, and reduce expenses by 80 percent.
4. Train the next improvement person. It is difficult to make great improvements through individual small improvements. The company should train someone to see the overall picture and plan the next improvements.
5. Establish a corporate culture based on a stronger ability to manufacture.
6. Be aware that companies can fail at any time. It is difficult to base JIT on half-hearted desires to do better. The

desire must be acute.

The Ise factory, with many issues yet to resolve, had still not implemented JIT. For them, Takahashi recommended the following specific improvement topics:

1. Pursue more rigorously the concept of "the subsequent process pulling work."
2. Make further improvements to those workplaces where work cannot be done standing up.
3. Improve the quality of movements. All operators should discover the wasted operations in their jobs and find a way to add value.
4. Adopt the attitude that producing a single defect is severe enough for sirens to sound throughout the factory.
5. Improve the still slow changeover times between products.

After expressing his thanks to Takahashi, President Ishizawa concluded the conference. He remarked that a report conference like this does not seek simply to report the successes experienced thus far, but rather is a forum to create topics for the next improvement activities. "We should each shoulder whatever load we can carry," he said. "Fall in love with the products you are in charge of. Sleep with them for a night. We are entering the age when we must question what true value is and make our products with the world in mind. The battlefield is the marketplace — go out there and wage an all-out war."

As I was leaving to return home, Ishizawa stopped me and said, "Come back for a visit next year. By then we will form lines for unit products and create sweeping, integrated continuous processing lines that can run small lots of all product types. Once that is accomplished, we will have made great strides forward in market-driven manufacturing."

CHAPTER FOUR

Dissension and Unity Between New and Veteran Workers

Yasuda Industries

The Depression Caused by the Strong Yen

It was around 1986 that we first heard that the loading docks of the world were heaped with machine tools. And in 1987 machine tool manufacturing hit rock bottom.

Examining the total Japanese production of machine tools for a five-year period, we find the following statistics (from "Statistical Study of Production Trends," Ministry of International Trade and Industry [MITI]):

- 1983: $2.92 billion
- 1984: $3.67 billion
- 1985: $4.37 billion
- 1986: $3.74 billion
- 1987: $2.86 billion

The machine tools industry, which had been steadily recovering from the oil shock, finally realized a long-cherished hope by recording a production volume of more than a trillion yen. Although a trillion yen is less than the yearly sales of a single large company, for the machine tools industry, which is a collection of mid-sized companies, this level was significant. Even the large manufacturers that sail the waves of business cycle recessions "that are sure to come every five years" gave a contented sign in 1985.

After the G5 "Plaza Agreement" in September of 1985, however, the sudden rise in the value of the yen and the trade frictions with various countries in Europe and America caused sales in 1986 to drop to about $3.75 billion, dropping further into the $2.5 billion range in 1987, the same level at which the industry had been seven years earlier.

The September 30, 1986, issue of *Japan Industrial News* reported the following:

> Total orders in August for the main twelve machine tool companies were $135 million, down 29.7 percent from the same time last year. This is the largest change over last year seen so far, results reflecting the tight market conditions for the second half of this year.
>
> The orders break down as follows: Domestic demand accounted for $84.6 million (a 33 percent reduction), and exports accounted for $50.8 million (an 11.3 percent reduction), and, as usual, the pace of downward motion was controlled by the poor orders received from clients. Although many manufacturers in the machine tools industry embarked on creating systems to reduce production by 30 percent, with orders dropping every day, many corporations sought ways to ensure survival despite further production reductions. Adding this to the further cooling of domestic demand caused by the strength of the yen and the problems with liberalizing restrictions on export to the United States, there were unfortunately no signs of any favorable changes in the export environment.

At that time no one could forecast that the industry could return to its level of $3.33 billion of the previous year.

The outlook for Yasuda Industries was also bleak. According to Managing Director Toshinori Sanada, "We were unable to consider increases in efficiency of capitalization or of management on a mid-range time horizon — we were completely involved in thinking only of what we should do on a day-to-day basis. Because we knew that slipshod methods would not be adequate, we did our best to come up with strategies to ensure our survival. Both employees and management came up with ideas for the company."

Skilled Handwork Still Exists

"Mother machines" are machines that produce other machines. For sixty long years, Yasuda Industries had produced nothing but machine tools. Sometimes, time-honored tradition gets in the way of progress and change.

In 1929 the former president, the late Shinjiro Yasuda, father of current company president Yoshihiko Yasuda, started in Osaka to make apertures in automobile parts, having developed a boring machine in 1928. Although the company had a temporary hiatus at the end of World War II, production resumed in 1946, and since then the company has been making high precision machine tools to open holes in parts. The machines produced by Yasuda Industries include honing machines and boring machines.

A turning point had come. The wave of automation and conglomeration pressed hard into the machine tool industry, and companies did whatever they could to transform their products into machining centers. From that time forth, Yasuda Industries came to be known as "Yasuda Machining Center." Having relocated from Osaka to Okayama Prefecture, locating its headquarters factory in Satoshō, the company maintains a work force of some 200 employees. Because of the great emphasis on software research and development, only about 70 of those employees actually work in the factories. Of all manufacture, about 60 percent is subcontracted.

The company's philosophy regarding technology emphasizes precision. A constant temperature is maintained throughout the year in the assembly plant to create an environment where sub-micron (less than 1/10,000 millimeter) unit accuracies can be produced.

Yasuda Industries takes great pride in the fact that traditional skills in making machine tools still exist. The parts that require the most precision in making machine tools are table surfaces, guide wires, and spindles. The level of precision is ensured in the final finishing processes, the scraping operations, which are performed by hand by the skilled workers.

In early 1988, representatives from Renault, Ltd., the French automaker, visited the factory on a study mission. After seeing the scraping operations, they returned home amazed that in this day and age there still existed this sort of journeyman work. No other machine tool manufacturers in Japan today perform these types of fine operations.

Scraping is a process in which any protrusions on the surface of the metal are planed away using a long knife-like tool, an operation yielding high degrees of surface flatness. Although formerly this operation was performed by hand in a time-consuming, painstaking process on the slide surfaces of machine tools and parts that required special levels of precision, today companies that perform the scraping processes are on the verge of disappearing. Craftsmen skilled enough to perform the operation are no longer available — and the precision levels of planers and other machine processing tools have increased.

"Everything is made to order — no two machines are alike, and the large machining centers take several months to build. We need to automate through computerization and mechanization. However, as is seen by our scraping operations, when the equipment cannot give us the precision we need, we will keep using the old techniques," says production department manager Kenshi Yamamoto.

A man who understands well the machine tool industry is Higashi Miura, a researcher at the Machine Promotion Association's Economic Research Center. His evaluation is that Yasuda's meritorious service brought the precision level of the mother machines up to the level of the production machines.

"We Can No Longer Manage Through Superficial Measures"

An old saying holds that "The third time is the charm." The JIT movement in Yasuda Industries was the third major companywide movement performed by the company.

In 1983 the company brought in a consulting company and embarked on a movement to raise the efficiency of its clerical and management work. In 1984 to 1985 a materials requirement planning (MRP) computer-aided production control system was implemented to rationalize the production control system. This was prior to the recession caused by the strong yen. I spoke with Managing Director Sanada:

> Looking back at it, our thinking was faulty. We thought to bring in larger computers to somehow package our production control work. But the assumptions of the time were that unless we had a philosophy of batch production — and did not change tasks once lump manufacturing orders had been issued — our efficiencies would certainly not improve.
>
> We now have moved, however, in a direction not at all anticipated. Fundamentally, we must be able to respond to customer demands. We came to understand that it is impractical to be locked into forecasts.
>
> Some machine tool manufacturers are as much "make-to-stock" as companies in other industries. But our company is completely "make-to-order," so there is no choice but to implement the particular desires and modifications of the customers.

The company gave up MRP and invited the JIT Research consultant Kenji Takahashi to visit their company. Like it or not, they were determined to implement the just-in-time production system, a system diametrically opposed to their previous production systems.

And the yen continued to rise in value.

"Because everyone was convinced that in taking only superficial measures the company's continued existence was endangered, we established a very bold objective." The company set a goal to reduce the five to six months that it takes to make a machining center to two and a half months.

The company determined the following promotional strategies and directions (*hoshin*):

- The establishment of objectives and progress checks would be done in a top-down manner.
- Objectives established through the promotional program would be accepted with tolerance, and immediate action would be taken to work toward the objectives.
- Individuals would start working toward objectives in their immediate work areas.
- Any activity yielding poor results should be corrected immediately.
- Individuals should contribute their own wisdom — those who do not contribute knowledge and ideas should contribute labor and perspiration.

The company president served as the head of the promotion committee, with Sanada as the managing director. Departmental and section managers served as assistants. The slogan of the movement was "Action — not complaints!" And "Y-JIT," Yasuda's production revolution, was set into action.

A Revolution in Awareness

The most important part of the promotion of Y-JIT was the revolution in awareness, a revolution soon seen in all occasions and in all places.

- Slogans were gathered and posted where all company employees could see them.
- Meetings were held to explain the movement in the various departments, including machining, assembly, materials, and so on.
- Baseball caps advertising the movement were distributed to all company members.
- JIT meetings for all employees were held fifteen minutes before the start of their shifts.
- Deliberate changes were made to the work environment through *seiri* and *seiton* (proper arrangement and orderliness).
- Project team members were sent on study missions to other companies and presented reports upon their return.
- Formal suggestion forms were distributed to all company members to ensure a full "improvement awareness."
- Intermediate reports were presented by company functionaries.
- "Awareness revolution" meetings were held in assembly workshops where there was resistance.
- Meetings were held with the assembly and materials management to explain the implementation of "Objective: 2.5 months."
- Changeover improvements were addressed by the machine shop managers and the production engineers.

- "Improvement corners" were established in the factories to display the details of improvements and scrap.
- Magazines, booklets, and pamphlets about factory improvements were distributed to all sections.

These methods made up the path that was followed in this awareness revolution. Because of concern with any variability in the awareness levels between the various work floors, horizontal communication was important.

A formal suggestion system was promoted with a slogan contest and awards for the best improvement suggestions. Although the number of suggestions gradually diminished after the program was begun, the quality levels of the suggestions rose.

Cutting Production Lead Time in Half

The primary objective of "Y-JIT" was to cut production lead time in half.

Sanada, the field commander who personally lead the program, explained:

> Yasuda Industries manufactures completely to order, with absolutely no "produce-to-stock" type of manufacturing to forecasts. There is no choice but to shorten production lead times so that we can respond agilely to the market. We implemented JIT with the thought that we could manufacture in half the time that it used to take, and that by shortening our lead times, we could adapt to customer needs even when they requested modifications, thus eliminating our computer-based system structure.

If you think that these actions were daring, you are right.

Changing to One-Piece Pull Production

Besides making possible the transition to a one-piece production system, the following changes also clarify inventory conditions in the processes, how to eliminate inventory and stock, and how to reduce late deliveries:

- Intermediate inventory levels were reduced as far as possible by running optimally small lots and by replacing the traditional "push" system with a "pull" system where workers from the subsequent process go to the preceding process to pull from it the parts that they need.
- Thorough instruction was performed with an eye toward reconciling awareness pertaining to operations for flow manufacturing.
- Signs and indicators were utilized to clearly define the storage locations for work (processed and in-process), tools, equipment, and so forth.
- A "warehouse inventory withdrawal control board" was instituted to schedule withdrawals from warehouse inventory (such as installment deliveries to assembly or painting workshops).
- The "daily production schedule board" and "daily assembly schedule board" were created to show the appointed production levels and actual results.
- A "multiskill control board" was created to cultivate multifunctionality (cross-training).
- Pallets and large-sized parts were made into "model parts" that performed "one-piece manufacturing."
- Signs were displayed to explain and implement JIT in the entire machine shop, beginning with the model parts fabricating processes.

"Visual Control" and "Schedule Control" were Practiced Through Displaying Signs in the Factory

The display of signs in the factory brought about the reduction of wasted time, the ability to see on-the-spot production conditions, and a heightening in the desire to achieve objectives.

Shortening Production Lead Times Through Installment Deliveries from the Warehouse

- Through supplying the assembly process (the final process in manufacturing) on a "just-in-time" basis, total production lead time was reduced.
- Parts for the spindles were delivered from the warehouse on a daily basis.
- A "warehouse withdrawal control board" was made and displayed so that installment deliveries would be possible.
- Warehouse withdrawals were separated by type of units.
- A list was compiled for installment deliveries of all parts needed up until the point of internal wiring.
- Installment and parts deliveries were synchronized.

Through these steps, the loss of time spent searching were eliminated in the assembly operations. Also, because large quantities of parts were no longer being delivered all at once, the company could get by with smaller parts storage areas. Being able to track the assembly process (through the "assembly daily control board") enabled the work to be controlled — from parts deliveries to final assembly — in daily units. At the same time, the gap between parts flows in both supplier and assembly sides disappeared and flows were connected.

The key to the success is the "assembly process board," which comes up in conversation time and again.

"It would be no exaggeration to say that this board was everything to us," said Production Manager Yamamoto. "First of all, this assembly process board shows the daily schedule of the assembly step, the final process. It is meant to

control all schedules based on the final assembly schedule —
reconciling materials deliveries, parts processing, painting,
warehouse deliveries, and so forth — showing to everyone
what parts should have progressed how far by when. In our
long experience in making machine tools, until that point we
had no methods to schedule people. Because of this, there
was some resistance from the factory-floor people wondering
why we were suddenly deciding their schedules. Therefore,
we weren't able to immediately implement the system. To us
it seemed that our being able to somehow overcome this
obstacle was a clean break with the past."

In clearly establishing the flow between the supply side
and the assembly side, the company had overcome a major
hurdle. Furthermore, as the operators became aware of delivery lead times, they were able to eliminate late deliveries.

The "Missing Parts List" to Reduce Missing Parts

In the past, there would always be parts missing when it
came time to start the assembly operations, creating the need
to perpetually pester people for the parts. This was the problem behind the "missing parts corrective action."

Accordingly, the delivery dates of the missing parts and the
names of the responsible parties are written on a list that is
affixed to a warehouse delivery cart. At this point, the reason
for the stock-out is investigated and corrective action plans
instigated to prevent them from recurring.

Layout Modifications

In order to reconcile schedules between the "fitting together
work" and other work on the unit assembly floor, the factory
was rearranged so that subsequent processes could see each
other. The results were improved communications, a reduction in distances traversed to pull parts from the previous station, and space opened up.

Through converting the polishing machines to a U-line, flow manufacturing became possible. Workers moved from being responsible for multiple pieces of equipment to being responsible for multiple processes — and grasping time, stop time, and inventory were reduced.

How the Consultants Evaluated Their Efforts

"Y-JIT, Part 1" commenced on October 29 and ended in March 1987. The difficult five months had passed too quickly, but the results were momentous.

- The objective of reducing lead time for the manufacture of one machine to 2.5 months was nearly achieved.
- The stock of materials and parts, including intermediate inventory, was radically reduced.
- Manufacturing costs dropped 15 to 20 percent.
- The factory performed the first two of the 5S's: proper arrangement and orderliness (*seiri* and *seiton*).
- A positive, aggressive attitude toward formal suggestion activities emerged.

"One major result was that, to a degree, there was a revolution in the awareness that if one tries, one can succeed. The workers adopted an attitude of 'let's try it and see,' even when the task looked difficult at first glance," said Managing Director Sanada.

In contrast, during this period the management environment in the company took a step in the wrong direction. Consultant Takahashi concluded the movement with his evaluation — and the score was unexpectedly weak. With ten points allowable for each of nine categories, Yasuda garnered only forty-nine points:

1. the method of promoting the activity (7 points)
2. the level of JIT understanding (6 points)

3. leadership (8 points)
4. inventory philosophy (6 points)
5. distribution of parts and materials (6 points)
6. equipment philosophy (4 points)
7. adaption of equipment (3 points)
8. flow manufacturing (6 points)
9. operations (3 points)

To Takahashi, who had performed similar diagnoses on automobile manufacturers, integrated electronics manufacturers, and leading large industries, a score of forty-nine might have seemed brilliant. Sanada, however, thought that Yasuda Industries had done better, as the first company in the machining industries to gain results from JIT despite the fact that the entire industry was "a legacy from the previous century." In reply, Takahashi pointed out areas for improvement, from top management down to the manufacturing floor, and made two general suggestions:

1. Top Management — make rounds of the work areas, devise a system allowing promotion team members to work more easily
2. Promotion Team — half of the team members should return to the workshops, improvements should be made by those on the manufacturing floor

Takahashi pointed out specific problems (some of which will be delineated further) to be resolved in the various work areas in order to further JIT.

On to "Y-JIT, Part 2"

The movement continued with "Y-JIT, Part 2" in April 1987. This time, a year was allotted for the long-term movement. In contrast to Part 1, which was dominated by younger employees, Part 2's promotion committee was made up primarily of higher ranking foremen and floor managers.

The slogan would be "Improvements Are Limitless" and the strategy and direction of the revised improvement activities would be shortening processes, improving changeovers, promoting multiple skills, shortening processing and assembly times, and reducing inventory — all based on the 5S's.

This time the JIT movement had a more definite objective structure than before.

Step 1: From May to July

- perfect the 2.5-month production lead time
- challenge the two-month production lead time
- reduce the intermediate inventory by $500,000

Step 2: From August to November

- stabilize two-month production lead times
- promote multiple skills
- improve changeovers

Step 3

- perfect two-month production lead times
- improve changeovers
- make the "multiskill challenge"
- reduce the assembly time of designated equipment types by 20 percent

The Movement to Improve Changeovers

One particular emphasis of "Y-JIT, Part 2" was improving the changeovers inadequately addressed in Part 1.

Improving changeovers is the most popular method in the implementation of JIT. The traditional manufacturing philosophy was to increase the lot size as much as possible, so that as many parts as possible could be made with the same setup.

In the age of large lot manufacturing, this might have been a valid strategy. Recently, the diversification of worldwide consumer needs has bred a new philosophy that optimal efficiency is born of running small lots — or even one-piece lots — through reducing product cycle times. This is a basic JIT concept; a main point is performing changeovers with adequate frequency to meet market needs. Previously, dozens of minutes — even hours — were needed to perform a setup change in a press or machining process. Now, however, innovations are needed to shorten the changeover times as much as possible.

The steps to improve changeovers are as follows:

Step 1. Categorize internal setups versus external setups.

Step 2. Convert internal setups into external setups.
Increase the amount of preparation that can be done in advance to expedite die changes and minimize the amount of internal setup work necessary.

Step 3. Shorten the setup time as much as possible.
To shorten setups, make improvements and innovations — including such steps as installing jigs, abbreviating the work of removing tools, performing standardization, and eliminating the removal of bolts (and the like) using cassette methods.

Step 4. Shorten the total changeover time.
Shorten the time needed to perform external setups. Combine this with shortening or eliminating the internal setup time in order to shorten the total changeover time.

Yasuda Industries, which has neither press processes nor plastic molding processes, embarked on a movement to improve machine process and assembly process changeovers.

Improving Changeovers in the Machining Shop

Takahiko Takemoto became the head of the machining section, which primarily performs machining processes. The machining section addressed the issue of changeover improvements during what they called "Period 1" (May to July) and "Period 2" (August and September).

Their objectives for Period 1 were to:

- perform proper arrangement and orderliness (*seiri* and *seiton*) on jigs and tools
- analyze internal setups, define internal and external setup tasks
- cut changeover time in half

Their improvement details and results follow.

Public Changeovers

Third parties (aside from the responsible functionaries) objectively analyzed the changeover operations, ferreting out wasted operations and allowing for improvements. This method of "public" changeovers brought over fifty improvements.

The Box Strategy

Through specializing the small parts (braces, receptacles, bolts, nuts, washers, and so forth) of standard products (from each process) and placing them in boxes on which the name of the user process was clearly written, the waste of having to gather the parts one-by-one for the next process was eliminated. This procedure was performed primarily in the large-scale product machining centers, and it assisted in improving the efficiency of the conversion of internal setups into external setups.

Supplementing and Providing Tools that Were Lacking

By providing additional tools to the machining centers, the wastes of changing and searching for tools were eliminated. This freed up people and reduced the non-value-adding monitoring operations.

Improving Transportation Carts

The work involved in handling intermediate inventory was reduced by 20 percent through placing stock items on carts as the work on each of the small items was completed.

Results of Creating Specialty Jigs and Improving Process Methods

- A jig for the indexing grinder shortened changeover time from 120 minutes to 40 minutes.
- A jig for the V-column process shortened changeover time from 40 minutes to 20 minutes.
- A jig for the top beam process shortened changeover time from 60 minutes to 24 minutes.
- A jig for the column feed process shortened changeover time by half.
- A jig for the saddle process shortened changeover time by half.

The saddle planing process, which previously had taken fifteen hours, was moved to another, operator-free process and shortened to five hours. Also, by developing specialty tools for the process that machined deep holes in tables, the processing time was reduced from eight hours to four hours.

Improving Changeovers in the Assembly Process

Creating Assembly Operational Process Documentation

Operator training was performed and assembly operations were standardized. The use and operation of measurement equipment and assembly tools were clearly defined. Through such measures, wasted operations were eliminated.

- In the operation of inserting the weigh plug, work time was reduced from 10 minutes to 5 minutes.
- In processing the front face of the induction scale attachment face, measuring time was reduced from 30 minutes to 0 minutes.
- Improvements in the method of cutting threads for the bed fastener reduced work time from 10 minutes to 5 minutes.

"During this period about 200 improvements were made resulting in a near 50 percent improvement. It is momentous that at last we are able to establish a production system capable of producing twelve units a month," said Yamamoto about the setup improvements.

Resistance in the Workshops

Changing methods established through long tradition is very difficult. Although many points should be raised in evaluating the results of the approximately one and a half years of the Y-JIT program (such as the increase in productivity and the beautification of the workshops), if we looked at only one point — a point wherein had there been no fundamental changes then the program would have been for nothing — then that point would be the attitudes and awareness of the technical and skilled personnel.

The dissension arising from the conflict with the old ways of doing things, the dissension arising from eliminating pre-existing concepts, was the largest issue for Yasuda Industries to overcome. The tension and friction was at a level unimaginable in most other companies. Of course, there is a history of floor-level resistance to manufacturing revolutions.

Value Analysis (VA) was developed in 1947 in the United States by Lawrence D. Miles at General Electric. This management method intends that the departments involved with sales planning, design, and manufacturing trace back and analyze functions, making improvements so that products having optimal functions can be produced at minimal costs. VA was used by the U.S. Navy and in 1955 was introduced to Japan where today many companies use it.

However, when Miles attempted to use the methods at General Electric, there was unexpected resistance. Even today the resistance from that time is known as the "Ten Articles of Resistance."

1. "That type of system will not be of any use."
2. "It might work there, but we are different."
3. "It looks good on paper, but . . . "
4. "Costs can't be reduced any further."
5. "But we already do that."
6. "It's not my job, so I don't want to do it."
7. "If we cut costs, quality will fall."
8. "Aren't we already doing OK? We don't need to change anything!"
9. "It's no good. We tried that twenty years ago."
10. "We're the ones who understand it the best."

Whenever there is an attempt to implement something new, reactions such as these from the floor-level workers occur. JIT, however, pays no heed to these objections.

JIT's Fundamental Attitudes of Improvement (Kaizen)

1. Eliminate preconceived notions about how things should be done.
2. Rather than explaining why things cannot be done, think of ways to do them.

3. Don't make excuses. First refuse to accept current circumstances.
4. Go ahead and move forward, even if the plans are not perfect.
5. Fix mistakes as soon as they occur.
6. Use the wisdom of ten people, rather than working for the glory of one.
7. When people say "I can't" or "I won't," the work does not get done.
8. Without struggles, one cannot become wise.
9. Promote the 5S's: proper arrangement, orderliness, cleanliness, cleanup, and discipline.
10. Improvements are boundless.

Although before implementing JIT the company established these philosophies by gathering everyone together and reciting them in unison every day, these concepts are more easily said than done.

Director Sanada said, "It's not that we didn't anticipate some resistance . . . " The resistance problems were not so simple that they would be resolved merely through appealing to references to the severity of the external competitive environment.

As an example, following the advice of the consultant Takahashi, the younger, more flexible employees were used in the promotion committee as a way to cause a rapid turnaround in awareness. As a result, older, more experienced people such as foremen and floor managers were alienated.

"The newer employees had never been on center stage until that time. Every day they had been thinking 'If I were running things, I'd want to do this,' or 'I'd want to do that.' Being in this frame of mind and suddenly receiving orders from the top to take the lead, they became arrogant. If you think that this led to friction between the younger and the more experienced employees, you are right," commented Sanada.

Confrontation Between Less-Experienced and Veteran Employees

As mentioned before, the assembly process control board was the deciding factor in reducing the manufacturing lead time. Once the order for a machining center is received, the schedules for the delivery of materials, for cutting orders for subcontracted parts, for processing in the factory, and for assembly operations are all determined in detail by this board. To make this board work, schedules must be strictly observed. To those employees who had been with the company for a long time, this regimentation of having to observe schedules was agony.

Another experiment was run, something not seen in the factory before. This was the attempt to have the employees develop multiple skills so that they could run multiple processes. The skilled journeymen, with the personalities of fine craftsmen, believed that nobody else could possibly perform the jobs that only they had done until that time. They attempted to protect their exclusive territories by building "walls" around their personal "fortresses."

In Y-JIT individuals chose the specialty skills that they would learn. The names of the workers and their progress in acquiring these skills were displayed on a board in the workplace. The three levels of proficiency were: "Intend to Learn," "Learned," and "Able to Provide Instruction." The skill board encouraged a sense of good-natured competition. The objective of multiskill activities was to provide everyone with the skills needed to run every piece of equipment, making it easy to cover for times where there was no work or no worker at a station.

The senior craftsmen were first to resist the new program.

"Since the old days there have been attempts to shorten lead times, but they have never worked out."

"I suppose it might work if we did it — but it's too much work and there will be more of a load on the workers."

"What happens when there are missing parts or defects?"

The more experience the employees had, the more they were able to read ahead. And the conclusion was quick in coming.

While the veteran employees were complaining, the young leaders were not silent either. At the same time there were adamant assertions from the top. It was imperative that they make Y-JIT successful. "Although we understand what you senior workers are saying, we are working as hard as we can on this and want you to do the same." Younger workers went around asking veterans for their help.

"It's strange. Once there were visible results, even those who had opposed the program assertively adopted it. Because all of the employees felt a sense of danger — that there was no tomorrow if one failed today — within two months from the time results first became apparent, the environment changed so much that it was unrecognizable," said Sanada.

In the reports of the Part 1 activities, these trials were apparent at a glance. "Through the six months of JIT activity, the project team members have felt keenly that even though things usually act as one would expect them to, people do not. They also felt that they wanted more time to work on the project."

When the last JIT meeting was held, one of the younger employees shyly approached Takahashi and asked for his business cards as a souvenir of this JIT activity. The consultant was touched and unconsciously held tightly onto the hand of the worker — it was a young man who had been losing his hair from all of his labors.

CHAPTER FIVE

The Factory Falls into Total Confusion

Shindengen Industries, Okabe Factory

On a one-lane highway through the rice fields stands a two-story white building. The rotary in the large vestibule is beautifully planted with shrubs cut to spell out "OSD" — Okabe Shindengen. This Shindengen Industries Okabe factory is ten minutes by car from the Hanazono interchange on the Sekie freeway, fifteen minutes from the Fukugaya station on the Japan Railways Takasaki line.

In many ways the hopes of all of Shindengen are pinned on this newly built factory, which, targeting the expansion of the electronics industry, began operations in April 1986. The plant manager at the time, Seiichi Tsuru, was entrusted with the plant when he was thirty-one years old. The average age of the employees is young — twenty-five years for male employees and just under twenty for female employees. The mission given to the strategic factory was to "make products that will fill the world."

The factory produces hybrid integrated circuits (ICs) for use in electrical equipment and semiconductor devices, electrical equipment for general use in two- and four-wheeled vehicles, electrical switching equipment for personal computers, office automation, and communications equipment, and so forth. Sixty percent of their products are electrical equipment, 90 percent of which go to Honda Technical Research Industries. As of May 1988 the factory had a work force of 223 people, including temporary employees.

The yearly sales of the company, indexed to 100 during 1986 operations, experienced remarkably rapid growth to a multiple of about 2.5 in 1987 (an index of 252) and almost tripling by 1988 (an index of 325).

Factory Revolution Through Eliminating Waste and Through the 5S's

The Okabe Production System (OPS) in Shindengen's Okabe factory essentially began on 7 September 1987. President Tsuru gathered all company employees to the second floor of the building and implored them to get involved in the OPS campaign. Although Tsuru spoke quietly, the content of his message was convincing.

> *The business environment today certainly is not friendly. Under the influence of the rising yen, many automobile manufacturers are moving to off-shore production. Competition between companies to increase their domestic market share is becoming fierce. In the midst of these factors, they are strongly demanding that our Okabe factory reduce product costs, improve functionality, and shorten lead times. Also we are asked to bring out new products. We cannot achieve these objectives without the strength of everyone who works in this factory.*
>
> *All employees must strive to create a corporate culture that is truly competitive and to actualize "total cost-minimized manufacturing," "timely, short-cycle manufacturing," and "high quality manufacturing" so that the customers are truly satisfied with our service.*

The company established the following objectives, based on June 1987 levels, with a completion deadline of December 1988:

- Increase value-adding labor efficiency (value added per unit of available time) by 30 percent.
- Reduce the intermediate inventory (in terms of number of one month's supply) by 33 percent.
- Reduce the parts inventory (in terms of number of one month's supply of parts) by 33 percent.
- Reduce the amount of late deliveries of parts from the current 20 to 30 percent to 2 to 3 percent.
- Shorten the production lead time by 33 percent (including paperwork lead times, receiving lead items, shipping lead times, and manufacturing lead times).
- Reduce defect rates by 50 percent.

Other indices were also selected: product stock levels (number of one month's supply of products), total corporate added value, sales volume per employee, capital productivity, and overall efficiency of machinery and equipment.

The essential conditions for the promotion activities were as follows:

- safety first — eliminating all accidents
- thorough 5S's
- eliminate all late deliveries and all customer complaints
- activities through the spirit of improvement
- visual control
- innovative creativity and improved morale

President Tsuru served as the committee chairman in the promotion system. The program was run in the following way:

An OPS general assembly would meet at four o'clock on the fourth Saturday afternoon of every month to ascertain general awareness about company direction and strategy, to organize activities, to check the state of progress, and to get an overview of improvement plans.

An OPS committee would meet at ten o'clock on the second Saturday afternoon of every month to plan the deployment of OPS, to establish plans, to prioritize improvement plans, to make project budgets, and to deploy OPS through the work floors.

OPS promotion group meetings would meet weekly to realize the actual work and to consider issues for improvement plans, internal public relations and the OPS campaign, and improving morale.

The program's slogan was "Factory Revolution through the 5S's and Eliminating Waste."

OPS News

Even before the advent of OPS, since January 1987, the company had been conducting the "Production Lead Time Shortening" program, a campaign with the theme of improving manufacturing efficiency through compressing the amount of work using production innovation. The program relied on people's spontaneous improvements — and participation was haphazard.

This time, however, the program was different. The revolution involved the entire company and all employees. The company thought to put out a monthly "OPS News," thus creating a single venue for the promotion of OPS. In early October, a month following the kickoff, the first issue of "OPS News" was distributed. Of course, the lead story featured Committee Chairman Tsuru's kickoff address:

> *When we all assembled in the cafeteria the other day, I explained the goals, objectives, and deployment plan of OPS. Some people are*

now wondering what precisely they should do. Actually, everyone must participate in achieving the goals.

I truly believe that we can achieve the objectives of:

- *increasing productivity*
- *decreasing intermediate inventory*
- *decreasing parts inventory*
- *decreasing late parts deliveries*
- *reducing defect rates*

This way we can create a competitive corporate culture in this factory that will provide service to our customers to their full satisfaction. Through this, we can improve the quality of human life.

In deploying OPS throughout the entire factory, we have selected two fundamental topics — the 5S's and the elimination of waste. In order to perform these activities, it is necessary first for shop floor units or individuals to gain an overview and to analyze current circumstances. Also, with anything that is done, it is important to adopt methods that have been successful elsewhere and try them here to see their results.

The OPS committee members, including the section heads, already have learned a lot through their participation in discussions, lectures, and off-site trainings. In the machining building the organization of space has already begun, and on the work floors the red-tag strategy that reveals unnecessary or unused equipment and products is already in progress. The 5S's and the elimination of waste, which appear simple at first glance, actually contain aspects that are very deep and involved.

At this point, with the world of manufacturing on the verge of change, let us strive together to use the joint power of youth and ideas to obtain superior results.

Factory Improvements Begin with the 5S's

The company took this challenge literally, and began with the 5S's. The theme of the activities was "5S's for production flow, 5S's for visual control, and 5S's for a cheerful workplace," echoing the concept that the 5S's — *seiri, seiton, seiketsu, seisō,* and *shitsuke* — form the basis for improvements.

The words *seiri* and *seiton* (proper arrangement and orderliness) have become the watchword of Japanese factories. However, the factories that have truly been able to perform them are few, with most only paying lip service to the concepts. Just lining up or restacking things isn't *seiri*, a word that implies straightening, organizing, and putting in order. It is only *seiretsu*, which means standing things in line. To be the foundation for improvements, the 5S's must be properly understood:

- *Seiri* (or proper arrangement) is discerning clearly between needed and unneeded items, and disposing of those that are not needed.
- *Seiton* (or orderliness) is organizing those items that are necessary in such a way that they are easily used, and labeling them so that they can be understood by everyone.
- *Seiketsu* (literally "cleanliness") supports the 3S's of *seiri*, *seiton*, and *sōji* (cleaning).
- *Seisō* is constantly cleaning.
- *Shitsuke* (or discipline) is developing the habit of always adhering to established conventions and practices.

Work Floors Progress Through Eliminating Waste

In September company members participated in field trips to other factories and in the "JIT Improvements Training Ground" (sponsored by the JIT Research Center). In October these activities were expanded to make improvements in the processes to eliminate waste and to create one-piece flow lines.

"Visual control" is a JIT process improvement method where management is attempted through the use of sight. It is a simple method in which decisions are made based on whether or not something can be seen or upon whether there are few or many of something visible, and a system wherein these decisions are tied to action. Visual control is primarily used in self-managed activities. It makes conditions such that anyone can readily spot problems or abnormalities.

For example, in attempting to reduce the amount of inventory between processes, one might limit special storage locations to hold only two or four units. If there proves to be fewer or more than that, the problem is readily apparent to both workers and managers and action can be taken at once.

Another method of visual control is the use of standardized parts buckets. Up until this time, various parts boxes were being used according to customer or type of part. In this system, however, it was never clear how many parts were included in the box or in what assembly those parts would be used. The people in the factory decided to use black buckets with the name of the factory clearly labeled for specific purposes:

- The buckets would be used only for the delivery of standard parts, intermediate process inventory, and work in process. The buckets would not be used for any other purposes.
- To the black buckets were attached fill-in-the-blank current parts rosters to be labeled as the buckets were used.
- The storage of readjusted goods was defined clearly with yellow tape on the floor marking the designated location of the buckets (yellow line indicators).
- Broken parts and broken work in process would be placed in blue buckets labeled "broken goods."

Other methods are that if problems arise on the production line, the operator can push a button to alert the manager or foreman to the situation. Or a factory might use the *andon* signal system of different colored lights that hang above the line allowing people to tell at a glance the state of the manufacturing floor and whether or not equipment and machines are operating or are stopped. Visual control might also employ a "production control board" that shows the state of operations at a glance. Or a company can opt to use "standard operations" to optimize the labor of workers, materials, and equipment.

JIT is easily accepted into a workshop and easy to understand because it has developed simple stepping stones like these as methods. It is based on standardization: standardizing operations, standardizing storage methods, standardizing inventory levels, standardizing *seiri* and *seiton*, and standardizing various other procedures found in the workplace.

Steady Progress

The OPS activities showed enthusiasm beyond anticipation. Although the improvement activities in the factory were only fragmentary, they still progressed.

The layout of the hybrid IC assembly line was modified. A movement to reduce waste started in the molding process with the use of buckets for carrying the interprocess inventory. In the process where the printed circuit boards are stuffed with IC's and other semiconductor elements, *andon* lights were added to the conveyer and soldering lines, and improvements were planned for the "baby-sitting" work in the inspection line. (This is where the operator does nothing but watch the equipment work.) Plans were made to convert the pre-shipping inspection process for parts inventory to "standing operations" (work done while standing up). The general affairs department addressed the themes of improving wasteful practices in dealing with paperwork and the ordering of office supplies, as well as improving communication problems between the administration building and the factory.

The area that saw the most progress was the electrical accessory product assembly line. The improvement objectives were the following:

- Convert the aggregate monthly production schedule into daily plans of the proportionate number of minutes the equipment is available per day.
- Convert to a system in which only one unit of intermediate inventory is allowed between the workers in the manual insertion process and the backing attachment assembly process.
- As much as possible, incorporate preceding work processes into subsequent processes.
- Establish a *"takt* time" (the optimally appropriate cycle time for the manufacture of each product). Have each worker resolve to manufacture one product within each *takt* time, calling the leftover time "idle time" (rather than using it to build another unit).

Thus, the company is on the verge of implementing various JIT methods — visual control, one-piece production and one-piece transport, *andon*, abolishing isolated islands, waste elimination, leveled production, and so forth — in order to switch from batch processing to one-piece flow production.

In only weeks, the company achieved a 200 percent improvement in productivity in the manual insertion process and a 180 percent improvement in the backing attachment assembly process.

"You Have an Excellent Way of Making Things!"

"Professor Hirano, will you perform a diagnostic examination of our factory operations? And don't hesitate to be frank about what you find. It is our intention to do whatever it takes to make this factory better."

A two-day diagnostic examination of the factory was performed by the consultant in November. Hirano's remarks were compiled from questions he asked during the examination.

In the warehouse:

- Looking at the automatic transportation system that runs in the plant, he asked, "What in the world is this? What does it take where?"
- Pointing to the parts shelves, he said, "This must be a joke! It looks like you have plenty of parts that will be used 'tomorrow.'"
- Looking at a storage location for subcontracted parts, he said, "Aigh! You have a goodly amount of supply parts, don't you? Any parts to be used, say, a month from now, are unnecessary at this time because the subsequent process is the customer. This storage method is wrong; classify according to manufacturer number."
- When he saw parts inspections being performed in lot units in the shipping inspection area, he said, "Collecting the parts before inspecting them is no good at all. Inspections should be performed in the factory — not here."

In the switching power supply manufacturing plant:

- Looking at a factory-floor parts storage location, he said, "How many people does it take to sort this stuff? When those guys stay home from work, who else knows the system?"

"There are a lot of buckets stacked here. What do you do when you need to get into the bottom one? What is stored in the one at the bottom?"

"You must thoroughly perform the 5S's. The company cannot be competitive unless the jobs can be understood and done by anyone.

- At the mounting process, he said, "There is too much space between the processes — make them no more than one meter apart. It takes four to five seconds to insert a part, but the operation is not really that difficult."

- Referring to the factory as a whole, he said, "Well, at any rate, you do have an excellent way of making things."

At the electrical accessories parts insertion process and circuit assembly process:

- Studying the manual insertion process, he said, "What happens when an operator doesn't keep up with the parts from all processes?"

- When he observed the test operations, he said "Where does this device go? What would happen if you put the tester before the coating equipment? Put some casters on the equipment and . . . "

- When looking at the front-end factory, he said, "It is unforgivable that the front-end processes are being done in a place like this. Make this operation and that operation as close as they can be to each other. At least open up some space at the end of the line."

In his two-day diagnosis, Hirano pointed out over a hundred areas needing improvement. Not only were all of the ideas new to the company, but they should have been obvious.

Factory Manager Tsuru felt the same way, "Because everyone in the factory was worked up over JIT at the time, the timing was excellent. Because problem areas were pointed out in specific terms, I think the factory will go along with him."

At this time Tsuru asked Hirano for direction on a monthly basis beginning the following January and Gotō was selected to be the visiting consultant.

From Vertical to Horizontal Multiprocess Operations

Just one week after beginning the OPS activity, a trial run of "one-piece flow production" was begun with the automotive electrical accessories parts. Process improvements began with eliminating waste, and the electrical accessories circuit plant was at the top of the list.

The following JIT methods and openings for improvements were established:

- *Visual control:* The month's production was divided into daily portions, and on any day only that portion was processed.
- *One-piece flow, one-piece transport:* In the manual insertion and backing attachment assembly processes, the operators had inventories of a single unit each.
- *Abolition of isolated islands:* As much as possible processes were connected — and preceding processes incorporated into subsequent processes.
- *Making a line where the waste is visible, and standardizing operations:* The company established *takt* times, and operators only made their allotted amounts (a single unit) within the allotted time. Even if there was extra time, operators would not begin work on another part — they would wait.

1. Improvements to the Layout

Taking the standpoint that moving around and transporting things is wasteful, the company removed the space between processes and tightened the connections between them.

2. Improvements to the Manual Insertion Process

The production line where the operators manually inserted the parts was a straight line. It was changed to a U-shaped line that is characteristic of JIT. *Andon* lights were set above the operators heads, and *mizusumashi* was performed.

JIT manufacturing emphasizes creating "flows" by using U-shaped lines. By changing from batch to one-piece processing, inventory can be reduced and products made without additional transportation.

"Flow manufacturing" is performing processes on each part in each of the manufacturing processes within the cycle time, emphasizing the sequence of the processes. In the past, similar processes were usually grouped together — all press processes, all welding processes, and so forth — grouping similar equipment in centralized locations. When operators ran multiple pieces of similar equipment, it was called "horizontal multiprocessing." This practice was eliminated in the company. Instead equipment was lined up according to process flows, with an operator running various different processes along the progression of the manufacturing flow. This method is called "vertical multiprocessing."

If a single operator is running heterogeneous equipment, and this equipment is lined up in a straight line, the operator must traverse great distances to operate all of the equipment. Moreover, if the group of equipment is being run by two operators and machine or defect problems arise, the operators cannot respond immediately because they will probably be working on a distant part of the line at the time.

In a U-shaped layout, the first and last processes run by an operator are as close together as possible. Using this type of layout for manufacturing, operators can be added or taken away as necessary in response to the manufacturing volume. In this situation, large-scale equipment is detrimental — compact, portable machines are required. Although it is often said in JIT that equipment improvements should be made following improvements to operations, JIT seeks simplicity in everything.

In JIT there are many interesting terms. One of these is *mizusumashi*, literally meaning "whirligig beetle." It derives from likening the operators swarming around a crowded factory to the whirligig beatles skimming around on the top of a pond. There are two meanings. One is two or three operators running multiple processes on a single manufacturing line. The other is in describing the operators, busily going back and forth between processes, carrying parts to ensure that defective parts do not get in the way, responding to problems in the lines, and performing setup changes.

3. Improvements to the Backing Attachment Assembly Line

Although the backing attachment assembly line is a process where parts are delivered from the preceding process and then minute parts are manually attached, there was a mountain of inventory between the preceding and subsequent processes. The preceding process virtually became an "isolated island." The situation was improved by creating a "one-piece flow" system that linked the processes.

As a result, the number of operators needed to run the manual insertion fell from 7 before to only 4 after the improvement, and the time taken to perform the process on one part was reduced from 11 minutes to 5 or 6. The same was true for the backing attachment assembly process, where the number of workers needed dropped from 8 or more to 4, and the time taken to process one part was reduced from 13 minutes to 6 or 7.

In these improvements, the first in the program to yield results, the productivity of the manual insertion process increased 200 percent within two weeks of beginning the process, and the backing attachment assembly process yielded a 180 percent improvement in productivity. Defect levels also fell and *seiri* and *seiton* were realized as well. At the same time, the workers, who until then sat as they worked, began performing their work while standing up.

Tadashi Kobayashi, the manufacturing department manager, featured these improvements as the top story of the third issue of the "OPS News" in an effort to draw the entire factory into the improvement program.

> *Although it is yet early, one-piece flow is being performed in Manufacturing Department 2. Shortened production times have brought large-scale increases in productivity and improvements in quality. Attempts do succeed. Fundamentally, the group had ambitious goals and a cheerful, energetic attitude of taking ownership of the activities.*
>
> *Transforming the workplace comes from transforming our own awareness. Therefore, each and every one of us must have problem awareness, use our heads, and have the unquenchable attitude of a challenger. We have youth on our side, and everyone is flexible. I believe that it is our responsibility as managers to use — and magnify — these characteristics.*
>
> *Although I believe that there are times when excessive demands and hardships are placed upon everyone, understand and be aware that only the fittest survive, through adapting to the changing circumstances.*
>
> *During this OPS movement, I ardently hope that each of you start by transforming yourselves. Along with that, I ask all managers, when making decisions, to clearly define who is to do what by when, and then to perform checks to make sure that it is done as planned.*

Through this revolution in awareness, the successes of the model workstation transformed the entire factory. What began as a point was expanding itself into a line.

Overtime Reduced to Zero in Two Months

Line improvements also began in Manufacturing Section 1. Operations Room 3, where components for automobiles engines were produced, had poor operational efficiencies that resulted in daily overtime. Two months after improvement activities began, the production room was able to produce adequate amounts of product without overtime.

This work area was a compound with ten operations: inspection, coating, assembly, soldering, drying, heat cycling, rinsing, final inspection, edging, and shipping inspection.

Improvement #1: Layout modifications

The space between processes was reduced.

Improvement #2: U-shaped lines

The series of processes from assembly to soldering were placed in U-shaped lines. These lines took up the same amount of space as the previous long straight lines.

Improvement #3: One-piece flow production

Prior to the improvement, there were parts buckets at each process, resulting in time wasted in verifying the numbers of parts and space wasted to place the buckets. By moving one part at a time, this waste was eliminated and production flowed smoothly and quickly.

Improvement #4: Operating multiple processes

The workplace personnel had a tendency to complain either that there was not enough production volume or that there were not enough people to deal with the volume. Therefore the system was changed to make each operator responsible for multiple processes.

Improvement #5: Standing operations

Running multiple processes contradicts what one might normally think — working sitting down actually becomes more difficult than working standing up. Eventually, all the workers decided to stand to perform their operations.

Improvement #6: Equipment improvements (the edging jigs)

Before the improvement, the pressure jigs would impact on the coated areas of the parts, resulting in areas where the coating chipped off and making rework necessary.

These 6 improvements resulted in a 145 percent increase in productivity. There were additional results in that the number of times that buckets needed to be pulled and replaced fell from 30 to 17, 58 square meters of production floor were opened up, the number of operators needed was reduced by 2, and quality defects (such as scratches and mars and incorrect items being mixed into the lots) were reduced. There were also other results, such as the elimination of overtime, which had consistently amounted to an hour a day.

The impressions of Hiroichi Komuro, an improvement leader, were that "because there was a strong feeling that production would fall into complete disarray and that there would be no hope of meeting shipping schedules, operators hesitated to undertake the improvement program. Once they set their minds to it, however, the results exceeded all expectations." The only failure was their initial procrastination.

Improvement activities and the 5S's were deployed in all areas of the factory.

Consultant Gotō used a favorite phrase, "Group the processes closer together!" in the Manufacturing Section 1's "clean room" (that manufactures hybrid IC's) as well. The results showed a reduction in the number of stagnate places through:

- minimizing intermediate inventory
- transforming operations where the operators are fixed in single locations to operations where the operators move between machines
- removing conveyers, shortening lines, and making U-shaped lines

Lines that had been 50 meters long were shortened to 20 meters, and overtime in the clean room was reduced by over 30 hours a month.

The Sound of Steady Progress

Since JIT was implemented in the company under Gotō's direction in January 1988, the work floors became nearly unrecognizable. In March, a Shindengen Production System (SPS) companywide report conference was held to review the previous six months.

President Tsuru felt that the business results of the JIT activities must be quantified in a form that everyone could understand. The quantification and reporting was the responsibility of the parent company.

Four indicators were selected to be used for JIT: (1) added value (productivity per person), (2) on-shelf inventory, (3) space cleared, and (4) worker rationalization. These indicators were used in all factories and on the section unit level to indicate JIT's progress.

By February 1988, added-value productivity had already surpassed the goals set for June of that year. The on-shelf inventory levels had been reduced to 0.35 months' inventory (nearing June's goal of 0.32 months inventory), 332 square meters of space had been cleared on the production floors, and six workers were freed for other functions.

"We don't yet have results that can be spoken of to other people, and we still have a mountain of things to do," admitted Tsuru.

Some optimistic data was delivered to President Tsuru — a graph compiled by the general affairs department of the number of requests for equipment modifications for the OPS program. As OPS progressed, the number of construction projects dealing with ducts, wiring, and so forth swelled. Compared to 1987, the number of construction projects had more than doubled in February and March 1988. Furthermore, the majority of the projects dealt with equipment and were run by the operators themselves.

Tsuru could hear the footsteps of steady progress.

CHAPTER SIX

Companywide Culture Shock

Miyamoto Manufacturing

The Production Revolution in the
Hitachi Parent Company

In 1978 the Hitachi Manufacturing Works, which had adopted the Toyota Production System after the first oil shock, initiated the "Minimum Stock, Minimum Stand Time" (MST) movement to quickly create an efficient production system adapted to the period of low economic growth. (This system is also called Hitachi JIT.)

The objective of the movement was to make products with the qualities demanded by customers in the quantities needed and at the time needed through the thorough elimination of waste.

In manufacturing, the true product cost is very small and is usually hidden by large amounts of waste. In order to discover the true product costs, wastes included in the costs must be brought to the surface and a rational production system fully established that thoroughly eliminates this waste. To accomplish this end, intermediate inventories, finished product inventories, and standard labor hours in manufacturing the products must all be minimized. This was the goal of the MST movement at Hitachi, where a management improvement movement had been in effect for nearly ten years. The MST movement was its extension into aspects of manufacturing and the largest companywide movement to date since it included all companies of the Hitachi group. Of the twenty-plus factories responsible for generating profits, some used the activity as an opportunity for a great crusade to control the fate of Hitachi in the 1980s.

The Sawa factory became independent of the Taga factory in 1968, having been established to specialize in the manufacture of automotive equipment. Its flagship products are automotive air conditioners, electrical accessory equipment for automobiles, spark plugs, carburetors, automotive exhaust elimination equipment, and other auto-related equipment. In order to succeed in the intense technical and price competition, and to perpetuate their positions as world leaders, automobile manufacturers ardently press to improve their manufacturing systems. At the same time they relentlessly demand of their parts suppliers improvements in cost, quality, and delivery lead times.

In response to the demands of the automobile manufacturers, the Sawa factory implemented a JIT production program called Sawa Action Plate System (SAPS) two years before the beginning of the MST movement.

SAPS began as an activity to improve machines and equipment. If we define the SAPS system as using the action plate method — which functions the same as the *kanban* system to significantly reduce inventory levels and to expose problem areas (tying them to improvement activities) — then always maintaining machines in a state in which they can operate at their full capability is a necessary requirement. This is the first area to which those in the factory turned their attentions.

Everyone Used Rags and Scrub Brushes

The first stage of the activity was the "530/450 (No Dirt/No Grime) Movement." Using the slogan "A cleaning is as good as an inspection," all activities in the factory were halted for a half day as the employees began to clean, using rags, scrub brushes, and mops, in an effort to purge the entire factory of garbage and dirt in a single sweep. Even the factory president participated.

Because of this unusual action, the eyes of Hitachi as a whole were on the Sawa factory. In the MST movement, which began later, the Sawa factory served as a model. This factory was ahead of the crowd, especially in terms of the uniqueness of the deployment of activities, ideas not found elsewhere, and innovations.

One particular innovation was an activity, begun in 1988, called the "Zenkigen Corps." The word *zenkigen* is a compound word combining abbreviations of several Japanese words with the implied meaning of "all company members demonstrating their full abilities." In order to provide leadership for subcontractors, and to deploy the MST philosophy into these subcontractors, project teams were formed as part of this program, and representatives spent seven to ten days with each subcontractor giving direction for improvements. Through this and other ways the Sawa factory led the other factories in their improvement programs.

A 30 Percent Drop in Sales

At that time, there was one small supplier for the Sawa factory that, according to the program, complacently made frequent deliveries of its parts every day.

"It seemed as if, even though the program really had nothing to do with us, we had to aspire to its lofty heights. Although we heard that the Sawa factory was giving direction to its subcontractors, our feeling was that they should keep their hands off our technology and off our organization," reminisces the youthful, thirty-eight-year-old company president, Yoji Miyamoto, who had inherited Miyamoto Works at the passing of his predecessor.

Miyamoto Works manufactures compressors for automobile air conditioners, with 100 percent of its production subcontract work for the Sawa factory. The company employs eighty-five regular workers and has yearly sales of $4.4 million (down from its $7.4 million of five years ago).

"The strong yen, the restrictions to exports, and the move to off-shore manufacturing have all placed a two- or threefold burden on automobile industry subcontractors. The greatest grief, however, is that the demands of the automobile makers vacillate wildly in terms of the types of products they require. Companies cannot ensure adequate work volumes," President Miyamoto explained.

Miyamoto was forced to implement JIT. He became interested in it when he heard a lecture sponsored by the Hitachi Regional Young Managers Research Group. This research group, composed of young second-generation managers, had a twenty-five year history of dynamic activities. On that occasion, they had invited Hirano of JIT Research to explain the nuts-and-bolts of improvement activities.

Miyamoto was aware that his company's parent company, the Sawa factory, was implementing JIT. He resolved to establish a production control system using action plates (AP's) or *kanban* between Sawa and his own factory. To Miyamoto, the remarks of Eiichi Tomobe, leader of the Young Managers Research Group and president of Ōtomo Manufacturing, played a decisive role.

An Unexpected Meeting After Ten Years

"Miyamoto-san, JIT will certainly have an effect. In two years it has completely changed what happens on our work floor."

"But would it work in a factory like mine? We've never done anything like this before."

"So doesn't that make it even better? Hirano was a friend of mine when I was a student — if you are of a mind to give it a try, you can ask him for help," said Tomobe.

Tomobe and Hirano had been intimate friends in school, where they had played in the school jazz band together — Tomobe on the trumpet and Hirano on the drums. They had hung around together and lived in the same tiny dormitory. In the ten years since graduation, Tomobe assumed that Hirano had entered the world of jazz music after graduating and Hirano thought that Tomobe had returned to Hitachi to inherit the family factory. While Hirano's prediction was on the mark, Tomobe was completely mistaken about Hirano, who since his teens had played with Sadao Watabe and other world-class jazz musicians from overseas.

Once when Tomobe was flipping through *Factory Management* magazine, he was drawn to an interesting article. Although he knew that the author was named "Hiroyuki Hirano," he never dreamt that it was his old friend. Even a year later, when Hirano's picture appeared in the magazine, it took Tomobe a while to believe that this was really the Hirano he knew.

"I gave him a call on the telephone. Boy, was I surprised! I flew to Tokyo. Hirano had become an independent consultant and had established a company. At his insistence, I called him in for consulting and he became our teacher," laughed Tomobe.

It was Tomobe who had invited Hirano to address the research group. When Miyamoto expressed interest in JIT, Tomobe was more than happy to show him the results of JIT in his own factory.

A Sudden and Substantial Drop in Sales

Hirano's direction began in November 1986.

"When a company is as far removed from the urban areas as ours, one has a hard time knowing what's going on in the outside world. I asked him in, if only to provide education for the top staff of the factory." The first six months was spent primarily in study groups with the factory manager, the section managers, and the section sub-managers.

Soon after the study began, however, a situation arose and sales dropped by 30 percent.

"In the beginning, I worried that the managers might not go along with Hirano. Then, just at that time, the company experienced a major downturn. Looking back at it, the timing was perfect. Had sales maintained the previous levels, there would not have been such a sense of urgency to make improvements, and it might not have been so successful," said Rikizō Nemoto, who had served the previous generation of management for many years as a member of the board of directors.

In 1987 the role of consultant passed from Hirano to Yoshimi Gotō. Slowly, JIT was moved into practice. The program was executed by first performing the "4S" movement of *seiri, seiton, seiketsu,* and *seisō* to make a clean sweep of all unnecessary items. As a result, two buildings in the Ōnuma factory, warehouses filled with inventory from four or five years back, were entirely emptied.

"Once the factory was spotless, it became far more conducive to work. In two buildings, we cleared out 150 square meters of space, which we turned into an improvement office, in one case, and let it sit idle, in the other."

Once the dynamic Gotō came on the scene, the factory made real progress in improvements. Once a month Gotō would arrive at the factory, touring the floor and pointing out areas requiring improvements that he called "homework." The people on the factory floor would somehow have to make improvements to these areas by the time of his next visit.

"Wasting all this money is no good at all" was a common saying of Gotō, who once worked in Toyota's engineering office. He would say, "Operational improvements should not cost anything. The point is to make improvements without money."

"Fundamentally," said Nemoto, "we had begun to eliminate unneeded items and to compact and to make operational improvements that were as inexpensive as possible. Although we had been engaged in improvement activities all along, the way we approached them had changed. In the past we considered the mere movement of our hands and feet as 'working.' Since the master has been with us, however, we have come to understand specific goals in shortening machine *takt* time, promoting multifunctionality, and so forth. I think that even the people on the floor have come to understand just what their real jobs are."

Make Equipment More Compact

As waste in the factory began to be reduced through operational improvements, Gotō resolved to progress to the next step — equipment improvements.

There was a bottleneck operation in the flexible hose process in the Ōnuma factory. In this process, hoses thirty to forty meters long were cut to appropriate lengths according to the types of cars that would use them. Although a machine to cut the hoses had been purchased from a particular manufacturer for several thousand dollars, the accuracy of the cuts was not as good had been anticipated, and the workers reverted to cutting them by hand. At this time an improvement made to the equipment not only produced wonderful accuracy, but also made the equipment more compact and only cost $300.

Another improvement made use of clothespins. The process in question was one where the hose was heated and fused to other parts. Although the process had been done with batch processing requiring the constant attention of an operator, a device was developed — with scrap materials and clothes pins — that used a merry-go-round-type system to gradually heat each piece one at a time and then automatically send it to the next process.

"In the past, we only did what we were told to do. Once this program began, however, we created an environment in which we assertively innovate. There is no longer room for excuses. In the past, when problems arose people would complain about not having enough workers. Times have changed and deadlines are always met. All of us — myself included — are experiencing an abrupt culture shock," laughed Miyamoto, throwing up his hands. "Because our company is constrained by the severe conditions of being a subcontractor that bound to a single parent company, in the future we will have to be flexible enough to perform JIT."

CHAPTER SEVEN

Teaching Flow Manufacturing on Sundays

Tateshina Manufacturing Works

- Manufacturing Era: "If you can make it, you can sell it."
- Sales Era: "Once you've made it, sell it."
- Planning and Development Era: "Make what you can sell."

The changing needs of the marketplace demand the production of small lots of a wide variety of products. If a manufacturer fails to establish a system that matches the circumstances of the times, that manufacturer will not survive.

"Adapting to the economic environment is difficult to do through simple measures. So the way management thought about the company and its production system remained as it had in the era of mass production. Everyone in the company was familiar with the phrase 'highly diversified, small-lot production.' When it came to manufacturing, however, products were made in batches with a great deal of waste. Merely knowing something is quite different than manifesting that knowledge through action," said Toshio Shimizu, production

111

department manager and a board member at Tateshina Manufacturing.

As of 1983, Tateshina Manufacturing had been unable to respond to its parent company's demands to cut costs. The amount of inventory necessary to support production in the factory was expanding, and the corresponding interest burden was becoming increasingly troublesome. The company could find no way to make a sweeping change in order to break free from this vicious cycle. It was firmly on the path to worsening financial performance.

"First of all, we felt the need to change the attitudes of all company members," continued Shimizu.

Through the efforts of Sunwave Industries, a Tateshina customer, the company began to hold in-house seminars presented by JIT Research in August 1983. This was the first step in its awareness revolution.

The company's economic conditions did not improve, however, and it found itself more and more mired in economic woes. Two decisions were made in December of that year: (1) essential production improvements were to be addressed as special projects and (2) an "improvement promotion office" was established.

Tateshina Manufacturing Works is a mid-sized enterprise located in the city of Saku in Nagano Prefecture. The company, founded in 1936, has a capitalization of $333,000 and employs, with its affiliates, nearly 300 people. Although for many years the company has produced and sold high-end furniture, manufacturing subcontracted woodworking for such companies as Sunwave, Toshiba Residential, Misawa Homes, Ōtsuka Furniture, and Sansui Electronics has become prevalent. The company has yearly sales of about $30 million.

The Improvement Objective Was to Eliminate the Need for Eight Workers

Improvement efforts commenced on 15 December 1983. Promotion systems were established regarding the production of cabinets and hutches for Sunwave. Grass-roots support was expected of all employees. Twelve support members were selected from the floor managers, section sub-managers, section managers, and department managers, emphasizing those personnel who actually worked on the manufacturing floors. The improvement support office was established under the direction of the company president.

Improvement objectives were as follows:

- Reduce head count from fifty to forty-two people.
- Reduce work-in-process inventory from four to three days.
- Reduce materials inventory from one month to six days.
- Reduce lead time from six to four days.
- Reduce operating space by one-third.

The summary and schedule of the movement were as follows:

- Promotion Method — First Phase Plan, January through March, 1984:
  - Mondays, Wednesdays, and Fridays were designated as improvement days and other concentrated improvement days were established.
  - As a rule, nonworking hours were designated as improvement time, during which improvement meetings were held and improvements executed.

- The second phase plan was from April to December, 1984.

• Improvement Methods:
  - *Exposing issues for improvements:* After a one-hour discussion, issues requiring improvements are chosen.
  - *Establishing issues for improvements:* Of the items requiring improvements, any that can be dealt with that day are promptly handled on the factory floor.
  - *One improvement per day:* At least one improvement was performed on each improvement day.

Floor Worker Testimonial, Shigeo Ōkuma
(Section Manager, Kitchen Furniture Section)

We had all grown up with the traditions of mass production systems. Once the equipment was set up, we would perform the same operations for a year or two without considering any changes. It was just the way we thought. Also, we disliked being pressured by the next process down the line, so we would build up a full day's inventory between stations.

When the number of product types began to increase, we divided up the month so that we would run each product twice. As the number of specialty products rapidly increased, however, we gradually reached the point where we were no longer able to increase production. Once we received our JIT training, we realized how important it was to eradicate our old, unyielding ways of thinking.

As we began learning, we decided to give JIT a try. We adopted the slogan, "If the results are not acceptable, go back to the beginning." Most of the department and section managers thought that had the company remained the way it was before the improvements, it would have failed.

By December 1984, people began coming to the factory even on Sundays — and even made presentations to their children about flow manufacturing.

One-Piece Flow Production

In what way would the manufacturing floor be changed? It was necessary to give all employees this sense of direction. The theme for the first phase of improvements was "Flow Production."

Just as the water in a large river flows smoothly, manufacturing processes must be such that each individual item flows smoothly through the processes. This is the basis of one-piece flow production.

This one-piece flow is one of JIT's most essential concepts. In JIT the flow is referred to as a "clean" or "smooth" flow. Flows such as those found in flash floods from concentrated downpours are called "muddy" or "turbulent" and are to be avoided.

In a clean production flow, one item is produced correctly to specifications each cycle time (that is, the time it takes to make the necessary items in the necessary amounts). In making products "just-in-time," the flows are critical. To achieve this one-piece flow, it is important to change the work-floor layouts, cultivate the workers' ability to run multiple stations, perform "leveled standardization" in orders, and so forth.

At Tateshina Manufacturing there was strong resistance at first to one-piece production. "Isn't batch processing easier and more economical?" "Hey, as long as we meet the schedule, let us do it the way we want to!" "If we're going to make the same product again, let's just make a bunch of them right now!" "Having a single operator run multiple processes puts a greater burden on the workers."

Floor Worker Testimonial, Takanori Kosuda
(First-Line Manager, Milling Process)

Suggestions about "What does it take to improve operational efficiency?" came from every area under my jurisdiction. First we thought of ways to shorten the time spent in transporting the lumber. We figured out where to put partially completed goods from vendors, researched processing times, and allocated equipment so that the processes would flow. People were reluctant, however, to depart from the way things had been done up until then. There was resistance to finishing one piece of lumber at a time.

Three Hundred Fluorescent Lights Were Eliminated

The company made improvements to reduce wastefulness in the factory. JIT Research instituted seven strategies for that purpose.

1. *Conceptual Transformation Strategy* (the waste of inflexible thinking)
   Let's get rid of any bullheaded thinking in the factory!
2. *Red-Tag Strategy* (the waste of clinging to unnecessary things)
   Put red tags on unused items so that waste can be seen at a glance.
3. *Kanban Signboard Strategy* (the waste of not knowing where things are)
   Establish designated storage locations and install signs to indicate where, what, and how many.
4. *Caster Strategy* (the waste of being immobile)
   Make it so that equipment can be moved when necessary.
5. *U-shaped Line Strategy* (the waste of equipment layouts that ignore operation efficiency)
   Convert straight manufacturing lines into U-shaped manufacturing lines.
6. *Multiple Process Strategy* (the waste of performing only one operation at a time)
   Promote the concept of operators running multiple processes, and have the operators learn multiple skills.

7. *One-Piece Flow Strategy* (the waste of large-lot production)
Pursue one-piece production, making a river flow
through the factory.

The *kanban* strategy requires more explanation. Once the
red-tag strategy is in place, only necessary items will be left.
In the *kanban* strategy, anybody and everybody can tell simply how many of what are left where.

Floor Worker Testimonial, Kiyoshi Morizumi
(Main Unit Drill Finishing First-Line Manager)

*The drilling group performs drilling operations, primarily using
boring lathes. Before the improvements, there was always a two- to
three-day stock between drilling and assembly operations. Today
that stock is only a half day's worth. Once we clearly understood the
work flow, our problems were diminished.*

In those three months following the December 15 start
date, more than adequate results rose from the steady efforts
of the employees.

- The head count was reduced by 16 workers, a 30 percent decrease.
- Work-in-process inventory was reduced from $52,000
to $30,000, about a 43 percent reduction.
- Lead times were reduced from 6.3 days to 3 days, a 52
percent reduction.
- At the end of the three months, 389 square meters of
space was freed up, 28 percent of the entire factory
- Using November 1983 as a baseline value (100 percent), productivity rose to 154 percent by March 1984,
roughly a 50 percent improvement.

As a result of clearing the space on the factory floor, the
need for 300 fluorescent light bulbs became unnecessary and

the heating bill for the plant fell significantly.

Floor Worker Testimonial, Zōnin Ōi
(Sub-Manager, Kitchen Equipment Manufacturing Section)

> *We can express the heart of the matter in just one phrase: "Improvements are not just writing things down. Neither are they just looking around or talking to people. Improvements take action."*
>
> *I asked around a lot looking for what had been improved and where, but I have found nothing that would explain a 50 percent improvement in efficiency. Perhaps it was the result of getting carried away with the red-tag and U-shaped line strategies. If we start to boast about how things have improved, however, we run the risk of quickly reverting to how things used to be.*

Phase one of the improvement activities had been completed. However, the activity had just begun. Shimizu, the man in charge of promoting the activities, made the following comments:

> *I think it is important that the people who have been involved in the improvements know the results of their labors, and that we tie these results into the next improvements. There are probably many companies in economic peril as we were, and people in such companies want their employees to know what we did to make our improvements — and save our company.*

The results of the second phase of improvement activities were even greater than those of the first phase.

CHAPTER EIGHT

A Survival Strategy that Brought Results in Six Months

Yonezawa Systems Research Group, Yamagata Prefecture

"The number of orders received here has fallen, and forecasts aren't very good either. What do we do now?" Although Takahata Electronics president Yoshio Suga habitually projects an air of optimism in his company, his face looked grave as he spoke with Director Takeshi Awa.

"That's true. It's said that VCR exports have fallen terribly. I've heard that sales for one of the large manufacturers have fallen by 50 percent, and that they have started to move people into their semiconductor departments."

Suga, also president of the Yonezawa City Electronics and Industrial Equipment Promotion Council, garners information about the industry from the top executives each time there are industry meetings. Although normally he makes decisions by himself, this time he wanted to hear the thoughts of the young Awa.

The Expected Industrialization of Post-Yonezawa Textiles

With the opening of the Tohoku bullet train, the city of Yonezawa had become close to Tokyo. It took only one and a half hours to travel from Ueno Station to Fukushima, and forty minutes from Fukushima to Yonezawa. Even by car the trip can be made in about three hours, entangling Yonezawa in the Tokyo industrial community.

Yonezawa is noted for its 200-year history of Yonezawa textiles, its Benihana dyes, its renowned Yonezawa beef, and is famous as the setting for the NHK (Japan Broadcasting Company) TV drama series "Oshin."

Yonezawa NEC, Hitachi Yonezawa Electronics, Meiden Communications Industries's Yonezawa factory, Tamura Electric Works's Yonezawa branch, Tohoku Pioneer's Yonezawa factory, Yonezawa Electrical Wiring — myriad companies seeking new frontiers have pushed into this land. And with them, subcontracting companies have emerged one after another. The region has the "Oshin"-type tenacity, and land is less expensive than that in the Kanto region near Tokyo. There is the problem, however, that the high-quality subcontractors cannot keep up with the sudden demand from top-notch companies. Add to this the adverse circumstances caused by the high value of the yen. In 1984, Yonezawa developed symptoms indicating that the "wolf cycle" was on its way — and that a downturn would follow.

The city, in the wake of the decline of the textile industry caused by the new materials revolution, placed high hopes and expectations on the development of the electronics industries. In the fundamental conceptualization to create a technopolis in the Yamagata Prefecture, the convergence of the electronics industries in Yonezawa was a fundamental pillar, with Yonezawa serving as an anchor. Over a hundred companies related to the electronics industry amassed in this region.

The Subcontractors' Barren Shelves

In 1983 the small and mid-sized companies who served as subcontractors to the large manufacturers in the area created, under the direction of Yonezawa City, the "Electronics and Industrial Equipment Promotion Council." With only seven companies of this council as the trigger, the "Yonezawa City Electronics Industry Conference" was born in 1984. In four years the membership swelled to fifteen companies, and with the aim of combining all companies in an effort to do something to improve financial results, the group spent three years in activities to improve operating environments. While thinking that it was doing well on its own, the group suddenly realized that it was not so. The world was changing rapidly and they were not keeping up.

"Mr. President, there is one thing I'd like to propose," said Awa to President Suga. "There is a very dynamic consultant in Tokyo. Recently I was reading about the just-in-time methods being used in the Toyota Production System."

"But would a teaching consultant come here? I don't think that Daiichi and Sharp are doing anything like this, are they? What I've heard is that Just-In-Time only works in the automotive industries."

"Recently, when I was in Tokyo, I learned that the consultant would be willing to work with five or six companies as a group."

"But, Awa, would he really be a benefit to the companies?"

"The consultant said that he was positive that his teachings would yield results. Regardless of whether or not companies are of the automotive industry or not, it is better for them to run 'just-in-time' than not to run at all."

At that time the internal conditions of the member companies of the council were dismal. The conversation went as follows:

- "We can't get supplies."
- "We can't keep up with the changes in the production schedules of the parent company."
- "We can't respond swiftly enough to design changes."

- "We produce one product type at a time in batch manufacturing."
- "There has been little progress in reducing defects."
- "This naturally leads to late deliveries."
- "Half of our factory space is taken up by inventory."
- "Even with the latest technology, there is a lack of control."

The problems were endless. However, worse than anything was the lack of problem awareness.

Suga was swift to convince the other company presidents of the benefits of hiring the consultant. "People don't listen to what others in the company tell them. It is cheaper if we combine ourselves into a group, rather than as individual companies, and apply for help from the prefectural and city governments."

Five companies, painfully aware of their current circumstances, were convinced by Suga's words. In November 1984, the Production Systemization and Rationalization Research Group (shortened to "Yonezawa Systems Research") was started by JIT Research. It had three objectives:

1. Free up labor and systemize procedures within the companies.
2. Improve and rationalize the production floors.
3. Systemize interactions with customer locations.

The word "systemize" appears twice in these objectives. What actually happened was not really systemization — it was "nuts-and-bolts, dirt-under-the-fingernails improvements" on the factory floors. Much must be done before something as elegant as a "system" can be implemented, and there is no real need to fumble with such "systematic equipment" as computers.

The consulting method was to be the following:

- Consulting was to be divided into "group training and leadership" and "individual leadership" and presented to each individual company.
- As a rule the consulting would be done once a month for three or four days for the next year, with between a half day and a day spent on group training and leadership and the remainder spent on leadership activities in the individual companies.
- The top executives themselves would serve as leadership role models to the companies.

To JIT Research, providing leadership through group consulting was a new experience. They were determined to make the consulting experience successful despite the unusual circumstances.

The following is an overview of the companies that received the consulting services (current as of April 1985):

- Takahata Electronics, Ltd.
  Capitalization: $593,000
  Production Levels: $296 million
  Number of Employees: 350
  Business: assembly of VCRs, color TVs

- Miyuki Precision Instruments
  Capitalization: $222,000
  Production Levels: $28 million
  Number of Employees: 250
  Business: manufacture of electronic and industrial equipment

- Union Electronics, Ltd.
  Capitalization: $55,000
  Production Levels: $18.5 million
  Number of Employees: 270
  Business: manufacture of electronic communications equipment

- Yamazawa Electronics, Ltd.
  Capitalization: $111,000
  Production Levels: $6.3 million
  Number of Employees: 100
  Business: manufacture of electronic equipment

- Ninomiya Electronics, Ltd.
  Capitalization: $7,400
  Production Levels: 22 million
  Number of Employees: 80
  Business: manufacture of electrical wiring and electrical equipment

Independence for the Subcontractors

The project did not appear to be very easy. Each company's products, technological levels, scope, and corporate cultures differed totally from one other. Observing the companies for a short period of time showed that they were not ordinary. A typical monthly schedule for the consultants was as follows:

- *Day One*
  12:30: Arrive at Yonezawa
  Afternoon: Provide leadership for Union Electronics
  Flow manufacturing of the automotive parts
  Create a U-shaped line where a single operator runs fifteen processes

- *Day Two*
  Morning: Miyuki Precision Instruments
  Improve the fax frame assembly process
  Improve line balancing
  Improve material handling
  Afternoon: Takahata Electronics
  Improve the color television assembly line
  Improve the use of both hands in inserting parts

Instantaneous equipment changeover in the adjustment process

- _Day Three_
  Morning: Takahata Electronics
  Company internal study groups (theme: _kanban_ system)
  Afternoon: Yamazawa Electronics
  Flow manufacturing of wire harnesses
  Improve the 4S's dealing with drafting boards

- _Day Four_
  Morning: Ninomiya Electronics
  Improve the plant circuit board assembly process
  Improve the methods of stuffing multiple board types
  Afternoon: Group training

This is how group consulting began in Yonezawa. Throughout the process, JIT Research promoted four themes in each company:

Theme #1: Make a production control system.
It would be wasteful to develop the same system independently for every individual company. Let's develop a system as a group.

Theme #2: Share improvement know-how between the companies.
Show how different people made things more rational. Exchange know-how about improvements between all members of the group.

Theme #3: Cooperate totally with the parent companies.
Get together with the customers and strive to create better products.

Theme #4: Produce better products by sharing information about aspects of the products.

If your own products are the most desirable, it is acceptable to investigate possibilities and look for a road to independence.

The Yonezawa Systems Research consulting, initiated in November 1984, yielded results beyond anybody's expectations within two or three months. Although each company in the research group had been involved previously in individual rationalization activities, because the activities were run on an internal basis and because the evaluations of the activities were also performed by people within the company, the deployment of the activities lacked intensity and rigor. The detail of the programs adopted by the separate companies prior to the group efforts also differed. There was a strong sense that their colleagues were also rivals. Although each company had its own parent companies, companies in the electronics industry traditionally don't know where their next work will come from.

Ninomiya Electronics — Starting by Eliminating Waste

Steeped in the local tradition and actually derived from the spinning industry, Ninomiya Electronics made the transition from being a textile company in 1969 to become a subcontractor for Yonezawa Electrical Wiring.

The following statement by President Kazuo Ninomiya motivated the company to join the systems research group: "Through a reexamination of the manufacturing processes we wish to create a corporate system that can respond to the needs of our customers."

Ten of the finest section managers, section sub-managers, and line leaders were selected from the manufacturing floor to start the "Ninomiya Study Group." This group began by exposing the various types of waste in the factory:

- copying waste
- shelving waste
- electrical waste
- transportation waste
- meeting waste
- equipment and jig waste

- changeover waste
- inventory waste
- human movement waste
- telephone waste
- rework waste
- redundant material waste

The study group determined to start by addressing three of the twelve: inventory waste, shelving waste, and human movement waste.

They first reexamined the processes by which components for facsimile machines were produced. The flow moved from parts receiving through receiving inspection, warehousing and storage, the assembly floor storage shelves, the assembly process, finished goods storage, the soldering tub, the lead cutter, repair/cleaning/backing, visual inspection, and shipping. By analyzing this long process in detail from the JIT perspective, the work involved in accumulation, value-adding processing, transportation, and inspections was understood as follows:

- number of times in the process where parts accumulate and sit: 25
- number of value-adding steps: 7
- number of transportation steps: 16
- number of inspections: 3

In contrast to the forty-four processes through which the parts pass and that do not directly relate to production (such as accumulation, transportation, and inspections), it was amazing that only seven processes added value to the components.

The study group then quickly moved on to the assembly process and eliminated waste by implementing the following methods:

- shifting inventory storage from the assembly floor to elsewhere
- eliminating the storage locations for assembled products
- moving the lead-cutter process closer to the soldering tub
- removing the shelves between the assembly and soldering processes

The improvement activities in the assembly process brought the following results:

Type of Process	Before	After
accumulation	7	7
value-adding	14	3
transportation	11	7
inspection	1	1

Through these improvements, the number of times that parts moved was reduced to less than half of what it had been. Previously parts, tools, and so forth had been scattered on shelves so that when it came time to work, they had to be sought for and found separately. After the improvements, placement locations and storage areas were clearly labeled and defined, making the human movements smoother. More than anything else, they came to understand that there is *muri* (unreasonableness), *muda* (waste), and *mura* (unevenness) everywhere.

Union Electronics — Initiating the Red-Tag Strategy

Union Electronics, which since 1983 had been running its unique "Union Power Campaign," participated in the systems research project with the objective of reaching even higher levels in its attempts to increase product multifunctionality, shorten lead times, reduce costs, and raise quality.

Its fourteen team members were divided into an improvement group and a production control system group. The improvement group determined to improve production floor operations by following five steps:

1. Verify conditions on the production floor and propose improvements.
2. Discuss integrated improvement proposals.
3. Create improvement plans.
4. Receive guidance from JIT Research.
5. Designate the next process to be improved.

In the midst of these activities, improvements were made to the mechanical parts assembly process, improvements that yielded great results. Major emphasis was applied, however, to improving the wasteful transportation system.

Improving Transportation Waste

There are three assembly processes for a particular product — parts assembly, mechanical assembly, and final assembly. However, the mechanical parts fabrication factory was some thirty meters from the mechanical assembly factory. Each factory was located in a separate two-story building and transporting parts required the use of elevators and transportation carts. The operations were in different buildings so that the component assembly operations would not encroach on the space for mechanical assembly.

The improvement group recalled the "Ten Improvement Fundamentals" advocated by JIT Research:

The Ten Improvement Fundamentals

1. Be flexible in thinking about how products should be made.
2. Find ways to make things work, rather than finding reasons why they cannot work.
3. Do not make excuses. Start by rejecting the status quo.
4. Do not seek perfection — 50 percent is fine for now, so take immediate action.
5. Correct mistakes at once.
6. Do not spend a lot of money on improvements.
7. If you are never bewildered or frustrated, then your wisdom will never rise to the surface.
8. Look for true causes. Ask "why?" five times to get to the truth.
9. Use the wisdom of ten people rather than the knowledge of one.
10. Improvements are limitless.

As a beginning point in seeking improvements, the group used JIT Research's "red-tag strategy." Red tagging is affixing red tags to parts and equipment thought to be unnecessary and performing visual *seiri* (proper arrangement) and *seiton* (orderliness). The result is that anything without a red tag is necessary and should not be removed.

Dejunking the Factory with the Red-Tag Strategy

It is difficult to tell what is necessary to the factory and what is not simply by wandering around the factory daily observing operations. When improvements don't progress, the reason might be that people don't understand what the problems are or what sorts of waste exist. It is necessary to perform operations to make hidden waste readily evident.

In the red-tag method of organization (_seiri_), red tags make "junk" (useless parts, equipment, supplies, and so forth) in all areas of the factory readily apparent to any observer. The six steps in the red-tag strategy are:

Step #1: Begin the Red-Tag Project.
- Get everyone to consciously perform the red-tag strategy on a daily basis.
- The program should revolve around the company president and "red-tag leaders" in the manufacturing, materials, control, accounting, and production engineering departments.
- Do not let the project last too long. One or two months should be designated as red-tag months.

Step #2: Establish the Targets.
- Define the work areas and products where the strategy will be applied. And remember — red tags should never be applied to people.
- Red tags may be applied to supplies, inventory, machinery and equipment, and even empty space.

Step #3: Establish the Criteria.
- Saying "Put red tags on anything that isn't needed" will not result in many red tags being posted.
- It is necessary to have criteria that make it easy to classify items as "needed" or "unneeded."
- Don't establish a grey area between "needed" and "unneeded." The concept of "when in doubt, tag it!" is an important rule.

Step #4: Make the Red Tags.
- The red tags should be highly visible. Make them, for instance, out of red paper or red tape.

Step #5: Decide on a Method of Adhering Tags.
- It is advisable to have non-management people tag the items in the factory.
- Management personnel often find excuses to hold onto items that should be removed.
- The people who perform the tagging must be ruthless and aggressive.

Step #6: Decide How to Handle and Evaluate Tagged Items.
- Inventory items should be categorized as defective inventory, dead inventory, accumulated inventory, and leftover (scrap) material.
- Defective inventory and dead inventory (inventory not claimed or used by anyone) should be disposed of as waste.
- Accumulated items should be sent to the red-tag storage area.
- Scrap material should be judged as to whether it is needed or not.
- Be sure to create an "unneeded item inventory table."

At Union Electronics, 486 items were marked with red tags as part of this project:

- warehouses: 383 tags
- machine shop: 93 tags
- manufacturing: 10 tags

As a result of these activities, when structuring the production control system, the company was able to systematically and smoothly adjust standard inventory levels. Also, because unneeded equipment was collected in a central location, space was freed up and improvements to equipment layout were realized. Finally, an entire department's floor space was completely cleared, resulting in the economization of support staff management.

Because the engineering and administrative departments were able to be combined in a single building, completely clearing out the space used by the engineering department, a long-standing issue was resolved — the mechanical parts assembly process was brought over from the separate building. This saved about thirty minutes each time products were moved in and out of the mechanical parts assembly process.

Improvement Activities at Takahata Electronics — Even the Consultants Were Amazed

In 1984 the export of VCRs, which until that time had experienced rapid growth, hit the skids. The demand for household electronics in general was also on the decline. Because Matsushita was in transition from home electronics to becoming an industrial electronics equipment manufacturer, the all-Matsushita "Action 1986" movement began in the second half of fiscal 1983. At that time the Matsushita Electronics and Chemical Headquarters combined departments in order to strengthen its home electronics division, and they deployed a program to renovate management through a "mixing of the blood." As part of this, all of the home electronics companies aimed for rationalization in a movement that included the subcontractors serving the Matsushita companies.

Takahata Electronics, which is the Matsushita subcontractor for the assembly of Sharp VCRs and color televisions, found itself in the unavoidable situation of renovating its own management. At the same time, because its size as compared to the others in the "Yonezawa Systems Research Group" was overwhelmingly large, Takahata Electronics was in the position to take leadership as the senior member of the group. Because of its role in inviting in JIT Research, Takahata wanted success at any cost. Also, because 70 percent of the company's production processes were performed by vendors, it was not only necessary to rationalize operations in the company itself, but the program needed to be deployed in such a way as to include subcontractors.

Creating a U-Shaped Line for Printed Circuit Boards

In the workshop where color televisions were produced, printed circuit board production and inspections were targeted for rationalization. Fifty employees stuffed the circuit boards and performed the soldering, finishing, and inspection processes. Changeovers between products, however, were terrible, and it was with great difficulty that the work floor responded to demands for multiple products. Could this line be converted to a U-shaped line? This conversion was the first theme adopted in the improvement movement at Takahata Electronics.

In the past, machinery and equipment were grouped by machine type or by function to facilitate the methods of large lot mass production. When similar functions or similar characteristics were grouped, inventory would accumulate in the spaces between processes, and great effort would be spent to transport products between processes. This sort of layout is called the "job shop" method.

In contrast to job shops, in the "cross-product placement method" machinery and equipment are placed according to the sequence of the process flow. This method is used for highly diversified, small-lot manufacturing and is called the "flow shop" method. As opposed to multiple equipment operations where operators run several similar machines in an attempt to rationalize the job shop, in multiple process operations a single operator runs several different types of machines at once in a flow shop.

Designing the production layout in a "U" shape in order to achieve multiprocess operations has the following merits:

- The layout can be changed according to the type of product.

- The series of processes for the product can be seen clearly.
- Because the entrances and exits of lines are close to each other, there are no wasted steps.
- Operators are able to assist each other.
- The layout is feasible even when space is limited.

In aspiring to make production lines that can quickly switch over between products, the operators (who are able to ambidextrously stuff components into boards) accepted the challenge to make a system where one line could be handled by a single operator. This was the first attempt at such a system in the electronic components industry. And the results were excellent.

Along with this, Takahata Electronics engaged in the 5S's program, eliminating fifteen storage shelves, freeing space, and making changeover improvements in the circuit board finishing processes and in the radio emission adjustment tests to products for export. The results were significant even during the early stages of the program.

The Workplace Where Personal Desks Were Eliminated

An example of an improvement that surprised even the consultants has special appeal to professionals.

Director Awa held the position of office support supervisor for the Yonezawa Systems Research Group. Because of this role, he developed a close relationship with Hirano and the other JIT Research consultants. He occasionally even dropped in at the JIT Research offices when he was in Tokyo on business. Being the kind of person who wouldn't return empty-handed from business trips, Awa always looked for some new idea to take back with him whenever he visited JIT Research.

"Mr. Hirano, won't you also visit the clerical offices just once? The people there are so diligent about improvements and they would be encouraged just by seeing you."

"I'd be delighted," Hirano replied. "But I wonder how diligent they really are in their attempts at JIT."

On his next trip Hirano visited Awa's production headquarters control center. He was amazed by what he saw — the office center had already made improvements that JIT Research's offices were only on the verge of implementing.

Factories always have volumes of documents and materials. Organizing and storing this paperwork is important. While a commotion always occurs on the work floor whenever parts are missing or when equipment breaks down, normally people in factories are amazingly careless when it comes to their control of documentation and paperwork. However, if this control is not executed properly, the rationalization of production will be flawed.

Awa gave his subordinates the following directions:

Step #1: Supply the necessary materials and documents.
Receive as many of the necessary reports as possible. If you tell people to cut back their reports, they will leave something out. This will cause problems and result in people having to write more than they might have otherwise. If everyone in the company did this, the situation would become intolerable.

Step #2: Purchasing.
Purchase less than you think you will need. If you run out, you can always buy more.

Step #3: Placement.
Be sure to establish the location where things will be put. Use the JIT method of visual control (a form of *seiton*).

Through repeating these three steps, the office was able to create a just-in-time environment in which items needed were used only in the amounts and at the time needed. This system is also applied to materials such as documents and forms. There is no need for more than two people to have identical items. Storage locations are defined clearly and items can be used in common by everyone. Through this manner of storage, the commotion that occurs when people are transferred, promoted, or leave the company is diminished — as is the need for extensive work in passing documents on to the next person assuming the position being vacated.

As a result, the need for personal desks was eliminated. The office created a system where all desks were considered community property. Anyone could use one — and not so much as a single pencil or piece of paper would be left on the desks.

Hirano, after his visit, returned to Tokyo with a very impressed look on his face.

The First Yonezawa Systems Research Report Conference

Although group consulting was a new way to provide JIT guidance, the earnest efforts of each company resulted in success beyond their expectations.

Yamazawa Electronics addressed in parallel both the 5S's and improving attendance rates. Due to increased awareness, in only four months the attendance rate increased 6.2 percent to a 97 percent level, and overtime hours dropped by 44.4 percent, or 1,430 hours per month.

Union Electronics successfully transformed its manufacturing system from an inventory-intense batch processing system to a flow manufacturing system. And although one department opted to remain seated while working, the rest of the employees moved to a system where they could work standing up. (Most of the companies, however, encountered stiff resistance from the workers to the concept of standing operations, so most were unable to implement that particular aspect.)

Miyuki Precision Instruments thoroughly analyzed its accumulation, transportation, processing, and inspection operations, intent on creating efficient production lines.

Team members zeroed in on the printed circuit board workshop where improvement operations often stretched late into the night.

"One day suddenly the equipment layout was changed. There were complaints that the new layout made the jobs difficult to perform and fatigued the workers. At any rate, because the changes were imposed on the workers from management, the workers had to be convinced that the changes were beneficial by living with them for awhile," said Yoshiyo Harada. Production volumes also fell temporarily, the result of over-confidence. About a week after the changes were made, the complaints stopped, and production volumes returned to their previous levels. In the second week, the company was able to remove five workers from the line.

However, there was a problem area. U-shaped lines were attempted in the Miyuki equipment workshops, considered the most promising work area because it was the only one in which the workers stood up. Unfortunately, there were many problems with workers getting in each other's way and productivity dropped abruptly by 50 percent. Being unable to meet its production schedules, after three days the lines were returned to their earlier layout.

After three to four months, the company presidents and the JIT Research consultants agreed to hold a conference and report the early success of the research group. In April, after six months had elapsed, representatives from the six companies gathered to report their various successes, the scope of which even the local newspapers and television stations covered.

PART TWO

JIT Overseas

CHAPTER NINE

A Strategy for Exporting JIT

Mitsubishi Trading Company Engineering Department

There was a heated discussion in the conference room on the fifth floor of Tokyo's Maru No Uchi Yaesu Building.

"Although until this time trading companies had only to sell things to earn their commissions, nowadays the major manufacturers are doing the selling by themselves."

"In the old days we were able to develop customers and distribution networks overseas, collecting fees for the value we added. But now, some manufacturers are working to slowly but surely develop their own markets."

"When individuals in our trading companies safeguard exclusive information, it is difficult for any company to have a systematic deployment of those skills. Under these circumstances, any sort of strategic management development is impossible."

"Whatever is said, we have been in the business of handling finished products in sales and distribution activities. But we need to go further and further upstream, pushing into the areas where the products are not yet built. Instead of only selling products, we must sell manufacturing, research and development, and management."

"Even when working on a commission basis, there are limits to what can be earned dealing only with hard products. Our merchandise of the future will be 'soft products!'"

"The large manufacturers already have distribution systems set up overseas."

This was the same old dialogue. The people attending the meeting had heard this discussion dozens of times before — not just in formal meetings, but in the bars as they gathered for drinks on the way home from work. Nearly ten years had passed since the company had crowned this decade as the "declining years of the trading company."

However, this time it wasn't just all talk. This was a meeting of "what should be done and how." It was to use the unique characteristics of the engineering department to determine specific new product offerings. As the meeting went on, more and more progressive ideas were advanced:

- "Let's assertively pursue high-tech work."
- "Let's do new business and new entry consulting, looking at restructuring industries."
- "Let's add technology transfer and incubator (nurturing of venture businesses) functions as well."

Mitsubishi Trading's engineering department secretly began, as a new business area, the "Technology Window Program," to promote technology transfers and the industrialization of high-tech work through a membership system. This new business area was to provide an intermediary for companies interested in high technology when it came to new business information and possible cooperative ventures. It also provided guidance for business plans, sometimes even plans extending into member companies and supplier companies. Working closely with its member companies, Mitsubishi Trading Company made full use of its network — a network with roots extending into all industries — and full use of the leading-edge technologies possessed by its engineering department. The network and the technologies were used in an experiment to provide guidance pertaining to the various problems that are central to management. These problems included dealing with the feasibility of industrialization, new product development, entering into new businesses, with market research, with production strategies, with sales strategies, and so forth.

Although when one speaks of an engineering department in a trading company there is a strong impression that its major function is to support the sales department, or that it is quite insulated from revenue-producing activities, the fact is that one of the major functions of the engineering department is to pioneer new business in areas dealing with technology. This was one attempt of the engineering department to create a product that offers to the outside world the know-how used by the department within Mitsubishi every day.

There were many meetings. Within the circle of people working on the project, one individual stood out.

Takeshi Hasunuma — managing director of Mitsubishi Trading Company's engineering department and member of the technology management team. Hasunuma graduated in industrial management from Waseda University in 1974. His emphasis was control engineering (or IE), and although of late it is not unusual to find members of trading companies with engineering backgrounds, IE specialists are still uncommon. His particular area of expertise, until then, had not been of much interest to the trading company. But now that changed. The customers of this program were interested in many of Japan's production (control) technologies.

Hasunuma, with his education in IE, pounced on their inquiries.

Although Japan's progress thus far has been based on introducing superior hardware (equipment) from America and then improving productivity, if someone were to ask if the root of Japan's having been able to surpass Europe and the United States in manufacturing was based entirely on hardware, the answer would be "No." Rather the reason for Japan's superiority was that TQC was the software (technologies) of manufacturing technology. When we started this project, we thought "Why not wait for awhile." There was no doubt that Japanese manufacturing technologies are targeted worldwide, so we researched that area.

The "JIT Boom" Overseas

Of the Japanese production techniques researched by Hasunuma, JIT was one of the most obvious. By that time, "JIT" had already become the watchword in the world of the experts.

The American Production and Inventory Control Society (APICS), is an organization that sponsors yearly meetings in all regions of the United States, attracting scholars and researchers in the fields of production control and manufacturing technology from all over the world. In the yearly general conferences of APICS, the amount of research and development pertaining to JIT was increasing yearly, to a point that might be called a "JIT boom." Books written by the consultant Shigeo Shingo and by Professor Yasuhiro Monden of Tsukuba University are being read in tens of thousands of company departments worldwide. The Japanese Productivity Headquarters and the Japan Efficiency Association receive requests everyday from people from many countries who want to visit JIT-run factories — particularly management from the automobile, electronics, and textile industries that have been vexed by Japanese competition.

Shigeo Shingo was awarded an honorary doctoral degree from Utah State University in the United States in June 1988.

For many years Shingo was in charge of educating floor workers at Toyota Motors, and was the pioneer of JIT, creating such terms as the "single-minute exchange of die" or SMED (reducing changeover times to under ten minutes) and "non-stock production" (the method of running manufacturing operations with minimal inventory levels). Six of his books have been published abroad, including his *Study of the Toyota Production System from an IE Viewpoint*, which has been translated and published in the United States, Germany, Italy, Spain, Brazil, and Yugoslavia. Shingo's name is known to managers throughout Europe and the Americas.

One U.S. publisher, Norman Bodek, president of Productivity Press, has an acute interest in Japanese management and control methods and has published, among numerous others, books by Taiichi Ohno and Shigeo Shingo. As Bodek says, "America is the birthplace of both quality control and the employee suggestion system. However, Japan has configured these methods to create something entirely different."

As Japanese companies have spread abroad, JIT rages like a whirlwind throughout the world.

Meeting with JIT Research

When Hasunuma considered using JIT as the seed for the growth of the new business, he thoroughly surveyed both domestic and foreign information on JIT, going so far as to travel to North America on several occasions. He honestly didn't expect to find as much interest in JIT overseas as he did, but when he discovered how much interest there was in the West, he set out to find a consultant who could provide leadership in JIT overseas.

Because he discovered that JIT is fairly well understood, he met diligently with many U.S. consultants, scholars, and researchers, looking for someone who would be qualified to teach JIT concepts. Although he found many Americans who had some understanding (gained through reading the literature or visiting Japanese plants) of simple JIT concepts, he didn't find a person who could actually provide guidance in JIT on a factory floor. For the management techniques in existence up until that time, it was adequate to merely report a book knowledge of the techniques. However, this is not the case for JIT — JIT requires the "dirt under the fingernails" methods that are centered on the factory floor.

"I assumed that because there was so much interest in JIT many people would be capable of teaching it. However, there were actually very few. Because this is basically a method that differs from the prevailing IE methods, the experts were naturally resistant. Nonetheless, Shigeo Shingo was providing excellent training in JIT overseas and was able to skillfully combine theory and practice in such a way that even foreigners could understand it."

A JIT Pilgrimage to North America

In November 1986, Hiroyuki Hirano and Kenji Takahashi of JIT Research, together with Hasunuma embarked on a two-week JIT pilgrimage to the United States and Canada.

The largest independent, nonprofit research organization in the world is Battelle Research Institute. This research center, based in Columbus, Ohio, was established in 1924 with the objective of becoming the world's greatest research and development, commissioned research, and education institute. About 8,000 researchers are involved in this institution, an institution that performs commissioned research following its motto of fusing scientific methods to manufacturing technologies in a broad range of fields based on (1) future trends, (2) regional territories, (3) system development, and (4) management development. Battelle's clients include governments or companies from ninety countries. Mitsubishi Trading Company's engineering department serves as the Japanese agent of Battelle Research Institute.

Battelle is also involved in assisting factory modernization and consented to a visit from JIT Research. For two days Hirano and Takahashi lectured on JIT methods and told "war stories" about their JIT Research experiences. Many researchers attended the lectures and asked questions about labor/management issues during JIT implementation, JIT's relationship to factory automation (FA), and so forth.

When the trio toured a manufacturer of industrial saws in Ohio and a manufacturer of dehumidifiers in Alabama, they saw signs of hopelessness and asked themselves questions such as:

- "How can we expect to see multifunctionality when the labor unions are so strong?"
- "Can we expect Americans to understand one-piece production when their managers are so locked into large-lot manufacturing?"
- "Will we ever gain strong cooperation from the factory floor?"

It was a visit to a Japanese automotive manufacturer's U.S. operations, a facility using JIT methods, that laid these worries to rest. Here both sports cars and compact cars were being assembled on the same assembly line. In one particular process where parts were affixed, fifteen different parts were delivered to the same hard-working operator.

In this factory, workers were hired only after they understood that work assignments were not fixed and were convinced of the concept of flexibility. The workers were assigned to fifteen-member teams, team evaluations were performed, and two teams could exchange at will the type of work they were doing. In other words, they were actualizing Japanese systems.

Hirano later admitted that initially they were unsure that they could make Japanese methods work in America. After seeing that particular automobile factory, their confidence grew. Hirano and Takahashi also provided practical guidance for shop floors, giving direction about various factory improvements for a sheet metal processor that is a California subsidiary to Mitsubishi Trading Company.

With the exception of this automobile manufacturer, the locations visited in this trip were mostly unaware of JIT. However, most managers knew that through applying JIT they could expect improved production efficiency, head count reduction, finished product and intermediate product inventory reduction, the elimination of waste in operations, and so forth. Most managers, in fact, were enthusiastic about implementing JIT. The three men were deeply impressed.

CHAPTER TEN

Facing Europe

Renault, Ltd.

The Voyage

Many opportunities opened for the consultants to travel abroad presenting seminars and providing leadership in just-in-time. This was due to the need that these countries had for JIT and because European managers had an expanded awareness of JIT. As an editor for a Japanese business magazine, I frequently received queries from overseas and I took great pains to help these people make contact with Japanese companies.

Although few Japanese consultants have stayed with foreign companies to provide long-term JIT guidance, Naoki Ueno is on a one-year-plus assignment in France with Renault, Ltd. He may be the only consultant to have provided such long-term consulting on the factory floor.

JIT Research's opportunities in France began with an encounter with a Japanese engineer living there. His name was Takuji Yoshimatsu. After graduating from Doshisha University, Yoshimatsu had traveled to France to work for

Japanese trading companies and Japanese automobile manufacturers. He joined Renault, Ltd. when he was twenty-seven years old and was put in charge of quality control. Later he left Renault to become an independent consultant. While on a business trip to Japan for the Japan External Trade Research Organization (JETRO), he came in contact with JIT Research.

When Yoshimatsu was with Renault, it already had a JIT promotion office. Although, to some degree, the staff understood JIT techniques, Yoshimatsu was aware that Renault had been unable to put them into practice. Determined to work with JIT Research to provide JIT leadership to Renault, he held talks with the company.

"Their JIT promotion department existed in name only. Although they understood JIT on paper, they had no consultants who could actually go onto the factory floor and instigate improvements," explained Yoshimatsu.

In the autumn of 1986 talks were held with Renault, a formal decision was made in December, and Ueno went to France in April. As supervisor, Hirano also visited two or three times a year.

The following "Letters from France," sent to us by Ueno and Hirano, record the struggles that these Japanese consultants encountered.

Ueno's "Letters from France" (Book One): The French Revolution

6 April 1987. In Paris we have been blessed with fine weather. Soon I will begin my improvement leadership to a French manufacturing company. The theme will be just-in-time manufacturing.

JIT is a production system that is practiced in its entirety only by a few companies even in Japan. I worry about how far companies in countries with different cultures and customs can progress with JIT, especially in France with its remarkably high level of pride in being progressive. I worry about how different human affairs are here, and I watch and take note.

Those of us providing the consulting services have already agreed that things will not progress as they do in Japan.

Regardless of differences in culture and customs, it is imperative that improvements (*kaizen*) begin with the 5S's. So we explained the *"cinq-S"* to the people here. In Japan such a discussion would be brief. We would only have to say, "The 5S's are *seiri, seiton, seiketsu, seisō,* and *shitsuke"* — proper arrangement, orderliness, cleanliness, cleanup, and discipline. The only thing left would be to apply the concepts to the factory floor. However, in France we had to explain what we meant by proper arrangement.

Many items on the factory floor are not needed there and this makes production more difficult. Therefore all unneeded items must be removed from the factory floor. This is "proper arrangement."

Following this explanation, we would hear, "Unneeded items? There is nothing unnecessary on *our* factory floor." Because of this we had to explain about unneeded things in the factory, and then explain the impact that "proper arrangement" has on productivity and cost. And then explain again. And again. At long last, we held the following interchange:

> "Well, *monsieurs*," they said, "let's start with *seiri*. And, by the way, because we're getting a contractor to do it, please set a date for it to be done."
> "A contractor? Why not do it yourselves?"
> "Why should we do it? Do you think we are janitors?"
> "Even if you aren't janitors, it is your factory and it makes sense that you should be the ones to clean it."
> "But we have work to do — we don't have time."
> "'Don't have time?' And you are supposedly members of the project team?"

If this happened once, it happened ten thousand times. In this country of strong individualism where job functions are defined with great precision, many things cannot be communicated even when Japanese-style idealism is found on the manufacturing floor. Also, directives of "Try it and see" are meaningless to them. Generally, their mode of operation is to forecast results beforehand and start work only when they receive authorization from the involved departments. With this type of procedure, people are able to hide from personal responsibility. The concepts of "Do it right away. If it's good, keep doing it — if there are problems, stop right away," and "Sixty percent is good enough for now. The point is to take action!" were unintelligible to them.

It seems as if the root of these problems is found in Renault's evaluation system and in sectionalism. Some might say that it is national character, but this is not necessarily the case. A number of people on the project team had an adequate conceptual understanding of JIT. I personally think the problem is with training.

Some members of the project team said that in order to perform smoothly what they were being asked to do would require an upheaval greater than that of the French Revolution.

It is said that France is a country where individual freedom is cherished. "Individual freedom" — words that certainly sound good. But these words are the villain.

When entering the factory floor in France, one is overwhelmed by the work-in-process inventory. No one even knows how long the production lines are. These are first impressions, impressions that would be felt by any knowledgeable Japanese associated with the manufacturing industry.

For the most part, the root to this problem of being overwhelmed and not knowing the length of the production lines is found in the attitude toward individual freedom. In this company, every worker — from the old Arab man who does the cleaning (for some reason most janitors seemed to be Arabs) to the company president — possesses this "freedom" in their jobs. But what is the freedom they claim? It seems as if it is the freedom to work as little as they want, or only when they want, regardless of the needs of anybody else.

Designers are free to choose what hours or days they want to work. And as long as the workers on the floor make the number of parts they are assigned, they are free to decide when to make them. This is called "free time" and accounts for 20 percent of the work time. Aside from this, there is the "allowance for operations" in the work. In this company, free time and allowance for operations total 50 percent of the work hours — meaning the rest is extra time.

And how is this time used? Set hours for starting and stopping mean that workers do not have the flexibility to finish up their work and go home early. Instead they use their "extra time" for coffee breaks, smoking breaks, and reading breaks.

When a feeder process in a production line falls behind, the first thing the worker does from the subsequent process is stop and smoke a cigarette. The same is true for an operator who has piled a large amount of work on the subsequent station. It seems that the more inventory that is stacked at the stations preceding or following one's own means more time for leisurely drinking one's coffee.

The labor unions uphold this free time and reducing it would be grounds for a factory strike. Because the companies have been unable to solve the problems of removing the potential for strikes, their costs are three times those of comparable Japanese companies.

It takes considerable time to change a company's work culture when that culture has been created over the span of decades. However, if that time of change occurs during an era of violence in industries and markets, then it becomes a time of self-destruction. Standing in Paris, where row houses have changed very little since the days of Napoleon, I am suddenly overcome by a sense of how quickly things change in Japan.

Although their manufacturing industries still lag behind those of Japan, the French are aware of the need for their own revolution and are on the verge of great changes. At present most workers still have only a vague notion of the danger they are in. Whether or not the populace that achieved the French Revolution can also accomplish the needed "Factory Revolution" will be revealed in the extent of its change in attitude over the next few years.

The First Improvement

The first areas over which Ueno was given authority were two large Renault machining plants on the outskirts of Paris and the Couronne factory near Normandy. These factories are in charge of fabricating engines and transmissions.

Upon preliminary inspection of the factories, Ueno was shocked at the length of the processing lines. He didn't know where to begin — the engine assembly line, an inflexible hanging conveyer line, was 1.8 kilometers long. Although Ueno wanted to divide the line into smaller manufacturing cells, he could not do it.

"Take a look at this line, everyone. You can't take in the entire factory with a single glance, can you? When you combine operations into a single location, control is simplified — and it is easier to make improvements."

Ueno began work to shorten this production line that could not be broken up. Because the 1.8-kilometer line could not be shortened physically, Ueno instead began such tasks as curtailing the rework areas while at the same time eliminating unnecessary cleaning machines. (When he asked what the cleaning machines were for, he was told that when the products came off the line, they were filthy and needed cleaning.) In the process, he combined the operational units into groups.

The truth is he had tried once before and failed. In Japan, JIT implementation begins with the 5S's. Naturally, Ueno also started with proper arrangement, orderliness, and so forth — but there was absolutely no reaction. It took him some time to realize that the 5S's were too difficult for the French automobile manufacturer.

The reason was that, even though the Renault employees understood the meanings of the 5S's, they had no concept of their necessity. Through compressing the processes and improving the way things are packed, people's jobs should become easier. For example, when grasping and releasing parts, if a worker doesn't know where the parts are supposed to be, the job becomes difficult. Only when people in the factory began to wonder what to do next did they begin to understand the necessity of the 5S's. Because of this, only after a year had passed and some degree of improvements were in process, did the factory begin to implement the 5S's.

Ueno's "Letters from France" (Book Two): The JIT Production System

In providing JIT leadership, consultants like myself must first make sure that the company understands the meaning and significance of compressing inventory and reducing lead times.

These people do not understand lead times. Moreover, from their perspective, they don't need to know because the concept does not enter into the company's evaluation criteria.

Each factory and each process is evaluated in terms of how many units or parts it produces each day. The question of how many hours or days did it take to make the units or parts is absolutely meaningless to the floor-level managers and production workers. Because of this, mountains of inventory surround the operators. In addition, because of the fear of equipment failures, mountains of inventory pile up on either side of the automated processes.

I am sure that it is because of the big difference in the manufacturing philosophy of Europe and Japan that the European automobile industry, which until about fifteen years ago should have been far ahead, has lost so much of its business in favor of Japan. While other factors do come into play, such as differences in labor practices in Europe and Japan, these factors alone can't account for the current gap between the two industries.

When comparing processing technology, I can't believe that such great disparity exists between Europe and Japan. When it comes to the skill in increasing the level of processing, however, there is a wide gap.

To perform similar work, many lines in this factory require lengths six or seven times those of Japanese factories. For example, in Japan if it takes a 50-meter line to produce a certain level of finished product, in this factory the same work would have to be moved 350 meters along the line. What happens along these additional 300 meters? Moving inventory back and forth, picking it up and putting it down, and other operations that tend to scratch and dent this work in process.

Although we established an immediate objective of shortening the production lines and eliminating inventory, we still have not managed to get them to commit to a deadline for its accomplishment. Although many issues remain unresolved, such as problems with the unions, there are indications that work has begun. Despite this, I think that it will be a while before I choose a French-made car for my family.

A Class-Conscious Society

Renault, Ltd., with its nearly 80,000 employees, is one of several government enterprises in France.

As Ueno said, "Maybe it's because this is Renault, but there are many areas in which JIT is hard to implement." First, there are the organizational problems. Yoshimatsu's statement that in France the people responsible for JIT don't go out on the factory floor is not entirely true — the fact is that they *can't* go out on the factory floor.

In the factories there are general workers — called operators — who work under the section managers and group managers. These managers are promoted from the work floor, and this level is the highest to which an operator can progress in the company regardless of how hard he or she works. Elite graduates from engineering universities, however, are promoted to section managers soon after entering the company, and promoted again in a year or two. With such little experience on the work floor, they cannot begin to understand the factory floor. This creates a vertical organization that is dependent on the educational history of the employees.

At the same time, there is a horizontal differentiation based on differences between departments. Renault has four independent groups for purchasing, quality control, production, and production engineering all within the production department. Each group has its own view of JIT, and according to Ueno, each has its own independent JIT promotion department. The department to which Ueno belonged was one with general responsibility for all of the areas — the production data processing department. This DP department, which uses computers and is in charge of general production control, is huge, with over 700 staff members. (Incidentally, it is said that of the 80,000 people employed by Renault, 4,000 are managers.)

Fortunately, the head of the DP department is a man who holds progressive philosophies, and his initiative and perseverance in JIT have borne fruit.

Hirano's "Letters from France": The U-Line Mountain of Inventory

"Monsieur 'Irano, we have made the U-shaped line that you had in mind, and we'd like you to take a look at it."

There I was in the French automobile plant. The section manager of the production floor, chest puffed out, broached the subject. It had been a year of hard work in the face of adversity. Now they tell me that they have made U-shaped lines. Impressive — considering that this is France and considering how large the company is.

During this year various things have occurred. Just communicating the concept of JIT was difficult. Wondering how to communicate terms such as *kanban, andon, poka-yoke* — to say nothing of *sarashikubi* (a head on a gibbet), it was natural to find our own heads on gibbets.

Although people think that many Japanese come to Paris, I'm sure that I was the only one who had his head on the gibbet against the background of the Seine River. It is very difficult for me to communicate here, and I have often wanted to throw in the towel and say, "Forget it — I'm going home."

Each time this happened, the Frenchmen in the department would try to calm me down by saying, "'Irano, please put up with us a while longer." When I think that, in spite of everything, they have reached the point of U-lines in only a year, I am nearly moved to tears.

As the production section head led me along, he told me of their trials while making the U-line, saying "We did this" and "We did that." I followed him around, nodding and saying, "No kidding?" and "Great," and "Excellent!" My heart was filled with a sense of satisfaction.

"Monsieur 'Irano, here it is!" he said confidently, with a broad sweeping gesture of his right hand pointing to the work area.

"Which one?" I asked, nodding slightly. "Which one is the U-line?"

I could not see this U-line in which he took such pride. I stared at the work floor, searching it over and over with my eyes as the section manager continued to point and say, "Here it is!" with pride and excitement. At first I didn't know what he was saying. The work area he was pointing to was a textbook example of a French large-lot workstation.

"That's nice — but I've already seen your large-lot work areas. Show me your U-line," I requested, not meaning to be insulting.

"But Monsieur 'Irano, this is the U-line that is the result of all of our efforts!"

"What!!!!" It came as a shock, and for a moment the room seemed to spin around.

"W-w-what's wrong???"

Looking very closely at the large-lot processing station, I began to see that the mountains of inventory had been connected up to make a U-shape.

"One pile, two piles, three piles . . . " As I counted the lots, I suddenly understood what the section head was trying to say. All they had done was to take their long, straight, large-lot processing lines and form then into U-shaped batch processing lines. Between the processes there were still mountains of inventory.

It was too ridiculous. I could not find the words.

He was expecting me to commend the line and was smiling as he watched my face. Although I felt like shouting in frustration, I reminded myself that this was not Japan — this is France. *France!*

"So, in France inventory is important. In making wine, if the wine doesn't sit for a long time, it doesn't become flavorful," I kept on telling myself. I forced myself to smile, but even I was aware that the look on my face was a bit strained.

"I understand that this is a U-shaped line. But because this isn't a one-piece flow line, there is inventory stacked between the operations."

I was calm and restrained to a level unfathomable in Japan.

"Monsieur 'Irano, we can't eliminate that inventory. If we do, the workers' freedom would disappear."

A country with amazing freedom — France. I didn't know that "inventory" was tied to "freedom." I turned to him and asked, "What is this freedom that you keep on talking about?"

He raised his left hand and started counting on his fingers, "First, the freedom to use the rest rooms. Second, the freedom to take smoking breaks. Third, the freedom to take coffee breaks. Fourth, the freedom to take rests. Fifth, . . . "

Well, fine. They will do as they please. They can count their "freedoms" all night long — and then they will have to live with them. It seems as if this factory has become drunk on the wine of freedom.

Strikes

At that time, the automatic transportation devices that were clearly unneeded in the transmission machining plant were eliminated. Also, in attempting to incorporate the equipment outside of the line that really should have been brought into the line, a strike resulted.

Another time, when I saw six people working in a haphazard manner, I instructed that they should be brought together to work in a one-piece-flow U-shaped line. When this was accomplished, the staff realized that the work on the line could be done with one less worker — so they removed a worker. There was a one-day strike in response.

While it varies from factory to factory, it would be no exaggeration to say that strikes are daily news. There was a six-week strike beginning in February 1988 to protest rationalization. Strikes also occurred over issues such as untidy bathrooms and getting their clothes dirty. Ueno sighed, "A strike would result if workers were asked to move twenty centimeters closer to each other to help shorten the production lines."

Therefore, we have to modify the way in which we provide guidance to the company. At Renault, things begin by forming groups. Consultants cannot go out onto the factory floor and say, "Please do this." While changes would be more easily accomplished were consultants able to demonstrate JIT concepts on the factory floor, we have no choice but to instruct the group leaders instead. Most of these leaders are section managers and group managers — only a few are operators.

"Because everything goes through the leaders, all instructions are indirect. If I try to do anything directly, someone from the organization pounces on me before the factory floor workers can even approach me."

In fact, Japanese walking in the factory hear shouts and jeers insinuating that they are behind the problems of rationalization and that it is not safe for them to be there.

"Although individually these people work very diligently, it seems that when they are organized they become violent. Because we cannot be too assertive in the factory, we do things like inspect the factory floor at lunchtime when people are out. There are times when, because of such situations, we just can't do our jobs."

With a look of hopelessness, Ueno said that it was because there were too many problems in the company before JIT was implemented.

Ueno's "Letters from France" (Book Three): Oh, Resistance!

Whether in Japan or in Europe, when one tries to change existing ways of thinking and acting, one always meets with resistance. Many factory workers feel that there is nothing wrong with their way of doing things — simply because they have done it that way for thirty years. However, because the world is always in a state of change, there are few instances in manufacturing where the same products are being produced using thirty-year-old methods and specifications.

Many companies who have clung to the past are no longer in existence. It can be said that knowing how much to change with the world flow is the key to a company's survival. However, keeping up with the world is something that is more easily said than done.

Whether it be a company or an individual, change is always painful. There is no doubt that people who oppose change outnumber those who favor it. Often people find that they cannot change even when they want to. A company is a gathering of people who are inclined to have these tendencies, and manufacturing floors in particular rely on past technologies and traditions.

Moreover, in Europe individualism is much stronger than it is in Japan. This respect for individual ways of life is seen everywhere. Even on the manufacturing floor, one is not controlled by the group — individual philosophies, jobs, and methods are respected. Many people would say, "Although the world is changing, I am who I am — don't bother me with other ways of doing things." Furthermore, France has a long history of resistance. This is a country that had such an active resistance movement during World War II that the German army grew quite weary of it. This indomitable spirit is seen in force on the factory floors.

I am in the seminar room in a particular factory. About thirty factory workers are with me, both operators and personnel from the equipment office. We are about to begin a JIT seminar. Everybody is looking to the front of the room, suspicion clouding their faces. The faces of a few people seem to say, "Hey, we've heard this *kanban* discussion before."

The discussion got underway and reached the stage of flow manufacturing. I explained the concepts of one-piece flow and lead times. Gradually the eyes of most people in the room began to glaze over. Suddenly, someone asked a question about the relationship between manufacturing lead times and the manufacturing pitch of finished products. Although there really is no relationship, this person was under the impression that in order to increase manufacturing pitch, lead times must be short.

In response, I explained using the example of an automobile's speed on a freeway. But there was no reaction. So I explained changing hands and changing products. Try as I might, I could not dissuade him from batch manufacturing. In the end it came down to the fact that he just didn't like flow manufacturing. For the rest of the seminar, he turned his desk to the window and stared outside.

It was April when the project got under way. The nine-member project team included five people from the production floor, one member of the headquarters production engineering department, and three from the factory control department.

The objective of the project was to design a line for the manufacture of a new product. Because the factory was fortuitously already producing a similar product, the plan was to modify the existing line and use the knowledge gained from manufacturing the existing product. As the discussion progressed, it seemed as if the representative from the engineering department was set on making a U-shaped line.

The section manager from the factory floor said that his operators were multiskilled and would be able to work in a U-line immediately.

With a "let's try" attitude, the project team had the senior member of the section's production engineering team make the drawings for the U-line. In French fashion, he drew the plans meticulously line by line and in the end produced a fine *U-shaped* line. It's true — it was a U-shaped line in shape. And so it was built according to this plan. The line had six processes in it and required three workers to run it — which is not good. If a single worker were to run the six processes, it would be fine. But in this plan, each worker has thirty units of partially completed inventory, allowing each to work according to whim. Upon careful examination, I noticed that there were X's between processes in the diagrams. When I asked the designer what they stood for, he looked at me strangely and said that the X's marked where the inventory was stored.

I mused on how they still didn't understand the JIT philosophy. After I lectured the work teams who would handle the U-line, and following considerable discussion, the project was begun again. It was August and the second set of drawings was finally complete. I knew that, despite my despair, I would continue to give seminars — and make them rework the drawings a third time. . . .

JIT French Style

We attempted to improve the changeovers of the wire harness installation process in the Belgian factory. In many factories, the workers become quite anxious at the thought of running multiple processes, at making U-shaped lines, and at anything else that threatens to change job descriptions and job skills or economize labor. Even though their workers may go on strike, however, even these factories are quite cooperative when it comes to improving changeovers.

During the period described, a changeover that had taken 90 minutes was compressed to 4 minutes. Interestingly, problems cropped up in dealing with the freed-up 86 minutes. The workers claimed that because the improvements were made through their efforts, they should be permitted to use the time however they wanted — not just for manufacturing. When asked how the improvements benefited the company, the workers could not understand that improvements should be part of their jobs. I'm afraid that it will be a while before these 86 minutes are eliminated from the cost of Renault automobiles.

Such situations reveal that JIT is interpreted differently in France. If the problems were just with words and language, they wouldn't be so insurmountable. Nonetheless the unavoidable fact is that the French theory of JIT is different.

The people of France rightly understand JIT as a set of techniques — U-shaped lines, *mizusumashi*, single-minute die changeovers, and so forth. When it comes down to why they are using these techniques, however, they can't really say — even though *supplying the items needed, when they are needed, in the amounts needed* sounds simple.

Take, for example, improving die changeovers. In Japan changeovers are performed so that the factory can move smoothly between product types, specifically making leveled standardized production feasible. The French, however, take a greater interest in the techniques that are used to reduce the total labor hours used for production. In extreme cases they don't even care about the fundamentals such as changeovers between product types and leveled standardization.

Ueno's "Letters from France" (Book Four): The Ardent Challenge of Monsieur Gerard

France has half again the land area of Japan, about 70 percent of which is flat. Its population is roughly half of Japan's. Aside from its several major metropolitan areas, most of France has about the same feel as the eastern plains of the island of Hokkaido. The high-speed freeways, called "auto routes," stretch to the east and to the west. And the starting point for everything in France is Paris, where distances are measured from the square in front of the Notre Dame cathedral.

All trains depart from Paris, heading out in all directions. Because of this, train travel is not the most convenient for consultants wishing to travel back and forth across the country because they must always return to Paris before catching a train for another destination. Everything either goes to or comes from Paris — it is the French transportation policy. Therefore I often travel by car.

I am on the auto route traveling east from Paris. We pass through the Champagne region and arrive at Metz. A little further, one can see the West German, Luxembourgian, and Belgian borders. It is a place about 330 kilometers from Paris. The feeling is very different here than in the factory outside Paris. Although the people here seem to speak French, somehow the language does not feel quite so Latin. While the people are indeed French, the Germanic blood runs thick in their veins. It has been three months since the improvement activities began and the pace has changed.

In this factory, production starts with forging the pistons. In another building, production begins with fabricating transmission casings and includes partial assembly. There were two improvement objectives: (1) to reduce the defects in the piston lines and (2) to reduce the intermediate inventory in the transmission casing lines. This does not imply that the area with the least inventory was the piston area — like the other factories in France, the inventories here are at horrible levels.

Initially, they investigated the causes of the defects. Even though the causes are already known, the research must be done. Here, the leading causes of defects are scratches and blemishes. When the finished goods are put in containers to be transported by forklifts, they are often scratched and dented.

First, one of the seven lines was selected as the model. This line made pistons for use in diesel engines. The line was divided into two parts, from the machining processes through final packaging. The machining processes formed an integrated line, and it appeared as if the equipment reliability itself would be a problem. Therefore we set out to eliminate defects in finishing.

When I asked, "Why is it necessary to transport these parts," the response was, "Because surfaces for use with diesel must be coated with carbon, they have to be moved to the equipment location."

When I asked, "And where is the equipment," their reply was "About fifty meters from the end of the machining line." When we went to look at it, we saw an enormous piece of equipment that looked like a steam locomotive set up on end.

I asked, "Is this huge piece of equipment really necessary to coat the surfaces of such small pistons?" The response was either dead silence or "We've used this equipment since the factory opened!"

"Well," I mused, "it might have been OK when the factory was first built but now this equipment is a problem." I told them to make a machine that could process one unit at a time and place it in the machining line. When I *ordered* them (as opposed to suggested), there were choruses of *"bonne ideé*!" (This would not have happened in Paris.)

The month after making the proposal, a prototype had already been constructed and was running on the line. Although various problems cropped up (such as dealing with ventilation), the factory people resolved them on their own. Currently the entire line, all the way down to final packing, is running one-piece production with no parts being transported out of the line for processing elsewhere. Naturally, scratches and dents have been eliminated and it is a truly effective machining line.

I think that in all of my consulting work in France, it was with this group that I saw improvement activities that were the most similar to those in Japan. Previously thinking that all European countries were alike, little by little I was being impressed with how different people are in different places.

When Ueno returned to France, he asked Renault's management some questions that are always asked JIT Research clients.

"We want to assist Renault in production rationalization and ask you to tell us what the company's goal is in terms of the level of rationalization desired through the introduction of JIT. Of course, we have goals that we would like to recommend . . . "

The French answered that, although they had no such goals, they would venture to say that it should probably be about 10 percent in two years. Of course, Ueno was astonished at this snail's pace.

It took the bewildered Ueno over a year to become accustomed to the French way of thinking and doing things. One difference dealt with the essence of JIT. Ueno became aware that the essence of this theory had some sort of relevance to the "freedom" that is of such importance to the French.

To begin with, just-in-time means synchronized manufacturing. It is predicated upon providing the necessary items with the correct timing. On the other hand, because freedom is based on not constraining people, it implies that all workers are asynchronous with anybody but themselves. This situation results in intermediate inventory being unavoidable.

There are also problems with equipment. During a period of nationalistic support for domestic manufacturers, Renault could not avoid bringing in inferior equipment. The result was poor uptimes and an abundance of equipment failures. Recently there appears to be a move to stop being so soft on domestic manufactures, with even nationalized companies such as Renault bringing in equipment produced in other countries — even Japan.

It is the same anywhere in the world. If the equipment is unreliable, the work floor becomes vulnerable. When this happens, people worry and respond by accumulating inventory. When people accumulate inventory, production lines grow longer and longer.

Ueno's "Letters From France" (Book Five): Does the Name Represent the Object?

France is wine country. Ducking into an intimate café on the way to work in the morning, one can see that the place is filled with old men who have stopped in on the way to work to savor their morning wine.

This time we will discuss the factory of Monsieur Gerard, who is the section manager of the transmission case machining and partial assembly line of the factory near Metz. Monsieur Gerard's group has been the quickest group so far in my consulting in France to understand (although only partially) and implement just-in-time manufacturing. This factory was just like the others we have discussed, with mountains of intermediate inventory on the manufacturing lines. But this work shop, perhaps because of the excellent education offered to the workers, was fairly clean.

The processes were broadly divided into fabrication and assembly. The fabrication side was typified by rows of large machines, with reliability, at that time, of less than 80 percent. The work traveled forty-five meters from the place where the line chief put it into the line to where its production was complete. We started by performing an "ABC" analysis with the goal of forming a line for the product type with the highest volume. Because it is expensive to move such large equipment, we started by moving the smaller machines about ten meters. They were placed in workstations in which the operators had enough extra time to run multiple operations. Next, we connected the line-off work between each process using roller conveyers, thereby eliminating the loading and unloading of the dedicated carts used previously to connect the fabrication equipment. However, because of the long distances between machines, inventory still accumulated on the roller conveyers.

Despite this, just through adding the roller conveyers, inventory was reduced from 4,000 to 1,200 units. Next, in order to eliminate inventory from the roller conveyers, we added limit switches to the roller conveyers, so that when more than one set amount of inventory remained on the conveyers the machines at the previous station would stop working. As a result, inventory dropped by another 600 units. In the fabrication line alone, inventory dropped to under 20 units.

Naturally, with the reduction in inventory, the station operators ended up with less to do. We really should have moved the equipment as close together as possible and reduced the number of required workers. However, the potential problems with the union — a fundamental weakness in the French system — made this impossible. We used the time that was freed up by having the operators perform self-managed inspections.

Then we went to work on the assembly process. The assembly process attaches a part dealing with the shift link to the transmission housing. The operations were performed "shish-kabob style," meaning that while each station performed its work, it would accumulate some amount of inventory before transferring it to the next station. In this process, however, each piece of equipment is movable. We compressed the line, which had been 15 meters long, into 8 meters, and created an inventory-free system in which operators were responsible for multiple processes. Because the operators were already multiskilled, the process was completed readily.

Finally, the balance of the line was not correct. Minor work overflows were dealt with by minor equipment modifications and by transferring work to the areas in the fabrication process where there was some excess capacity. Through this we were able to reduce the inventory in the overall line to forty units. Because reliability is yet poor, there remains some off-line safety stock. However, this group was exemplary in its progress in only two months since beginning the improvement activities.

Although there is still room for improvements, other lines in the company require attention. So, for now, we are establishing this as the model line and horizontally deploying its improvements to other lines. Not only were inventory levels on this line improved, but productivity rose 25 percent over the previous period and lead times dropped from 22 hours to 56 minutes.

Foreign Laborers

There are various reasons why factory rationalization is poor — reasons such as history, behaviors, attitudes, conventions, and systems. Top management also has a theory about why JIT doesn't go well. Although several times a year Renault sends people to Japan to study Japanese companies, there recently has been a change in the middle managers who visit us. This change is their feeling of hopelessness.

In March 1988, Ueno and Komatsu accompanied the Renault study mission. When asked their impressions, a member of the study mission replied, "We came here hoping to learn from Japanese companies that are doing well. But the differences are too great! I can't see how we can ever compete."

The member of the study mission went on to discuss education and training, the ability of the people on the factory floor to make improvements, and companywide unity in projects.

"I don't think that the abilities of the individual operators are in any way inferior to those of the operators in Japan," responded Ueno, but he pointed out a great obstacle to overcome. "Although the scarcity of labor is affecting both Japan and Europe, in Europe — and especially in France — the problem of foreign laborers has become profound.

"Bringing in foreign labor means dividing up work areas, work skills, and cultural and racial backgrounds. In Renault the distinction is clear — the French are management and the operators are labor. Regardless of ability, people who have had little education or opportunity to demonstrate their skills remain in the factory. At Renault, half the factory workers are of either Arab or African ancestry."

The circumstances make it impossible for "the wisdom of the workers" to be seen. Instead, there is confrontation. At Renault, "rationalization" means getting rid of workers. And people don't want to make improvements that will cost them their jobs.

Ueno also asked the members of the study mission about their impressions of Japan and things Japanese. "The way we see it, it would be dangerous for Japan to admit workers from other Asian nations. Look, for example, at the problems the West Germans have with the Turks. When France allowed in foreign workers, there was a scarcity of labor and the economy was such that anything we could produce would sell. France can still afford to use foreign labor because it is still resting on its laurels from when it was a powerful nation."

The problem is not only with foreign labor.

"It is said that in the highly individualistic France, there is no custom of viewing objects in their entirety. Managers don't think about what is good for the company as a whole. For them, it becomes important to demonstrate their authority. Because of this, important management information doesn't flow down through the organization. Of course, neither does information from the factory floor flow up the ladder."

Why doesn't information flow?

"If people tried to make information flow smoothly, they would violate the norms of the group — risking both their necks and dismissal. Because of this, people think it better to just do as they are told in their own little areas of responsibility."

We understand the *monsieur*'s feeling that "We can work all our lives and not catch up with Japan." It is said that in France it takes a year to make even a small improvement. This is because one must consult with the technical research laboratories.

The work floors examined by Ueno are only 10 percent of Renault as a whole. Even assuming that the work floors yielded results, they would have little influence on the company as a whole. As Ueno said, "I wish we could expand our scope from 20 to 30 percent. The workers in the shops where we consult have come to understand about 60 percent — but 40 percent is directed horizontally. And some of the people involved are highly motivated."

It appears as if it will yet take some time.

I remember what Hirano said, "When I go to France and visit the work floors, for the first week or so I wonder why it is that people in France work so little. But after about a week I wonder why it is that people in Japan work so hard."

After a long interview with Ueno, he and I went for drinks at a Japanese *yakitori* shop. It seemed as if Ueno was tasting Japan after a long absence. When his thoughts returned to the here and now, he said only one thing — "When viewed from there, Japan is certainly different." The next day Ueno returned to France.

CHAPTER ELEVEN

Korea's Thirst for Knowledge

Samsung Electronics

October 1987. A call came to JIT Research from Korea inviting Hirano to give a seminar there in March. In addition, the management at Samsung Electronics wanted him to inspect their factories.

Samsung Electronics is the top integrated electronics manufacturer of the Samsung Group, a group typical of Korean industrial groups — and typical of the Korean manufacturers that are taking bites out the market shares of the Japanese integrated electronics manufacturers.

This was not the first time that JIT research had consulted for a Korean company. Three years earlier, JIT Research had consulted for Keum Ho, a Korean tire manufacturer in the city of Kwangju. Although the original request was to implement a computer-based production control system, many problems needed to be resolved before the introduction of computers, so progress was slow and began with the 5S's. Initially, Hirano visited the company, followed by Ueno and Takahashi consulting once a month. Consulting ceased in 1986 because incidents in Kwangju and a move toward nationalization caused the site to be eliminated through rationalization. It ended, unfortunately, just at the point where they were about to see results.

Although in the past progress was made through introducing software along with the Fujitsu hardware, this time it was to be different in Korea. On March 23, 1988, Hirano departed Japan, armed with materials and high hopes.

The seminars in Korea began at seven o'clock in the morning, with top executives and management listening to lectures until nine o'clock while eating breakfast. It was called the management "morning exercises." Beginning in Pusan, Hirano presented seminars in four cities in three days.

The audiences were very responsive. About 90 percent of the people already knew about JIT and raised serious issues such as "Doesn't it annoy the subcontractors?" and "Doesn't it potentially intensify labor?"

Hirano visited a Samsung Electronics factory on the outskirts of Seoul. The factory employees 20,000 people in the manufacture of electric fans and VCR's. Vice President Lim, home appliance manager Chang, production manager Son, TV department manager Kim, and quality management manager Lee all met him.

To Hirano, who was accustomed to seeing the most progressive production facilities in Japan, the work floors of the Korean supermanufacturers did not leave a good impression. They were still batch processing and relying on hunches instead of rationality, and standardization was lagging. The production method concentrated on hardware and the actual product flow was not done well. A Samsung official on the production floor said, "When compared with the Japanese home appliance makers, we are running seven to eight years behind." Hirano mused on how this place was a diamond in the rough. As Hirano was walking out, quality management manager Lee tagged along and beseeched him to "give us guidance."

Hirano replied, "It will take at least three years, with the first six months devoted to education alone." Hirano was already thinking about potential programs for the Samsung Group:

- touring factories and pointing out problem areas
- conducting in-house seminars
- providing direction on how to make and implement improvements on the factory floor
- improving subcontractors and suppliers

Beginning in June, Hirano would be very busy consulting for Samsung Electronics.

PART THREE

The JIT Workplace

CHAPTER TWELVE

———

The Secret of JIT Is in the Workplace

Western managers do not trust knowledge gained from the workplace; hence, they believe that if they mechanize and automate, production will increase and product quality will improve. Unfortunately they too often adopt what Toyota calls the "big boat, big guns" approach — that the bigger the equipment, the better.

JIT, however, is improvement strategy for the workplace. In fact, the workplace is a trove from which many treasures flow. In his book *Workplace Management* (Productivity Press, 1988), Taiichi Ohno, whom we call the "father" of the Toyota production system, writes:

> It is crazy arithmetic that figures the effects of rationalization in terms of how many percentage points more rational things get every month. You may not see any effect of rationalization at all. Or you may see a sudden surge if production increases and that increase is accomplished without additional equipment or people. In some cases, results will lag most where small improvements (kaizen) are accumulated one by one. But even if you give up on

gradual improvement and bring in computers and robots, you will be unable to use them right away. This is why those daily accumulations must never be abandoned . . .

Although we use what are called "standard operations," the standards involved must be changed constantly. You should never think that standards are perfect. If something deteriorates, then the change is for the worse; if it gets better, then it is an improvement. Human beings discover which is which by chance, so it would be silly not to keep changing things.

An Emphasis on the Workplace Is the Lifeblood of JIT

The workplace is where things really happen, where the most important information is obtained, where the most immediate information — necessary for improvement — exists. Suppose an improvement strategy is based upon faulty information about the workplace. Such an "improvement" is not really an improvement at all. By the time information is second- or third-hand, it becomes distorted.

For this reason JIT leaders and practitioners constantly stress the workplace. A division chief of a large company said,

> *Usually when a consultant comes, the first thing he does is ask for materials. We sit in an air-conditioned office and go over the data, and when we are done, we hand over this analyzed data. A JIT consultant, on the other hand, will immediately go to the workplace, point to problem areas, and propose a plan for improvement.*

The number of people doing JIT consultation is small, but they all work this way. If you can't give guidance in the workplace, you cannot be called a JIT consultant.

The late Shigeo Shingo always carried a white hand towel in his pocket — even when in his wheelchair — because he expected to get oily. He also carried ballpoint pens with his name printed on them. When improvements went well, he gave them to the operators who were extremely happy to receive an unexpected gift from such a respected man. After observing this, a president of a large chemical and synthetics company always speeds to his company by car brandishing a bottle of Johnny Walker Black whenever he hears results of improvements. His efforts have been successful, and this particular company has experienced a large boost in morale.

When Toyota began spreading its production system to its affiliates, the company — using its automobile production research office as its base — started a Toyota Production System independent research group with the aim of actually getting Toyota affiliates to experience and master improvement technology. Toyota enlisted members from among its affiliates, and every month the group would visit member companies, both uncovering problem areas and moving the companies toward improvement.

As the name implies, this research group was only attended by companies (or individuals) who had a desire to participate, and so the activities were intense. Because there was a feeling that the Toyota Production System could not be realized half-heartedly, scenes in which leadership listened carefully to the man or woman on the job were frequent occurrences.

A process of pointing out problems and improving them before the next meeting would be repeated over and over. If the indicated improvement did not happen, there was work — with an intensity that might lead late into the night — until they saw an improvement. Difficult, perhaps, but the results kept getting better. It was so intense, that people had a saying: "Whenever the independent research group comes, ten people are cut from each line."

Using this method, Toyota attempted to saturate its affiliates with the Toyota Production System. Sometimes Toyota representatives would stay at a company for ten days to a month giving advice. "Through information exchanged in the workplace, the members internalized the Toyota Production System," says Tomonori Kumagai, an instructor at Nagoya Technical College. "The role that the independent research group played in establishing the Toyota Production System is inestimable."

A real place, real circumstances, and real objects are the three pillars upon which JIT stands.

The Man Who Loved the Factory

Tomō Sugiyama, once in charge of production at Yamaha, expressed the following: "To make good products, a company must have good leadership."

In 1982, after forty years, Sugiyama quit Yamaha. Now at the age of seventy-four, he flies around the country as a seminar and improvement guidance consultant.

Few men value or love the factory floor as much as Sugiyama. With no academic credentials, he was hired by Yamaha (presently Japan Musical Instruments Manufacturing), became a salaried worker, and through his efforts and natural abilities became a director. Even then, he cared about the workplace so much that he visited it every day.

Sugiyama's three rules for generating improvement strategies are:

1. Thoroughly scrutinize the situation for five minutes.
2. Make immediate notes of the 3M's: *muri* or unreasonableness, *muda* or wastefulness, and *mura* or unevenness (or variability).
3. Perform the 5S's: proper arrangement, orderliness, cleanliness, cleanup, and discipline.

Previously, with Yamaha in charge of production, Sugiyama had worked with Toyota to build a sports car, the Toyota 2000 GT. This car was considered a "dream machine."

Of the great influence Toyota had on him, Sugiyama notes, "I was in contact with Toyota's methods during every step from development to production. They differed from anything that I had ever seen and excited me in many ways."

Ways to Generate Improvement Strategies

Sugiyama originated his techniques and philosophy for workplace improvement out of these rich experiences. He argues that in order for workplace improvement to move ahead, the foremen must be improvement-minded.

> *The thing that we usually fear most is when people get into a rut. A person who has settled into a job over time becomes as contented as a frog in a pond. The next thing you know, that person has contracted "chronic job-rut syndrome." Dealing with this problem is hard, however, because the person is completely unaware of his predicament.*

Sugiyama instructs that to encourage improvement-mindedness among first-string supervisors you must do the following:

- Make them aware of the useless areas in their workplaces.
- To do this, get them to closely observe their workplaces.
- Give them a firm grasp of what is necessary to improve in their workplaces.

He continues, "If improvement-minded, a supervisor can work for improvement with the staff. However, if this awareness is missing, it is fatal and the supervisor becomes unresponsive to the plans made by the staff or others."

Sugiyama feels that single, small, companywide changes added together can bring substantial results. However that may be, people must develop the habit of generating lots of their own improvement ideas. With this end in mind, Sugiyama devised the "3M Memo" improvement technique to eliminate unreasonableness, waste, or unevenness. "It needn't be in the exact form of an improvement plan. It needn't be directly connected with improvement. Just take notes whenever and wherever you notice *muri, muda,* or *mura.*"

With this cry, Sugiyama led the successful rationalization campaign that followed the first oil shock. In recent years, the 3M strategy has been borrowed by Toshiba and Mitsubishi Electric in their rationalization campaigns. Overseas, it has been widely disseminated as the "3U Memo" — unreasonable, unnecessary, and uneven.

Again, Sugiyama says to thoroughly scrutinize the situation for five minutes. "Five minutes may not seem very long, but it is hard to stare at one place for five minutes. Do it, and you are bound to come up with an idea. It's almost certain." The third point in Sugiyama's offensive for generating improvement strategies is the 5S's.

"A problem is the indispensability of leadership ability in generating improvement strategies. Those with leadership ability also have a high level of improvement ability. Properly forging the wheel that steers the car is the secret to success in generating improvement strategies."

CHAPTER THIRTEEN

———

Developing JIT Improvement Specialists

Nagano Prefecture's High-Diversity
Small-Lot Production System Research Group

Surrounding consultant Kenichi Sekine is a group taking on the task of developing factory improvement specialists outside the framework of particular companies or industries. Sekine, another consultant who thoroughly pursues JIT, was the subject of a journal article I once wrote:

> *3 February 1984. Three and a half hours following my transfer to a Nagoya rapid transit bus, I am at Komagane, a city located roughly in the center of Inadani District. When I arrive, the short winter day is already at its close and I am thoroughly chilled.*
>
> *The man at the front desk of the business hotel smiled wryly. "Except for during the Komagaoka spring climb, this place is dead," he said. Having spent most of my time in large cities and in the industrial belt, I felt as though I were in the wrong place.*
>
> *Until recently, the place was considered undeveloped, even for rural Nagano Prefecture, but factories have expanded vigorously. The growth of high-tech industries, and the electronics industry in particular, has been remarkable. The prefecture attempted to stimulate enterprise within its borders and hammered out a plan for a "techno-highland" suitable for a highly informed society. The plan*

divided the prefecture into five separate blocks, and, as an entice-
ment to leading-edge technology companies, universities and
research groups introduced new media and provided a transportation network and a good housing environment. They attempted to
gather together leading-edge technology industries and so increase
the technological power of — and expand the amount of work coming to — small and mid-sized enterprises within the prefecture.
Copying California's "Silicon Valley," Inadani was called "Inadani
Techno-Valley."

It was after six o'clock when Yamaguchi, section head of the
industry diagnosis group at the prefecture's integrated guidance
center for small- and mid-sized companies, and engineer Shioiri
arrived. Kenichi Sekine, manager and lecturer for High Diversity
Small Lot Production Research Group, Kurasawa from Shinano
Specialty Equipment, and Ueshima from Tenryu Precision Tools
immediately joined the meeting.

Yamaguchi asked Shioiri about the results of current activities.
Ueshima said, "At first, I thought this would be little more than a
social gathering for company presidents and wondered what I'd got-
ten myself into now." Kurasawa added, "If I hadn't been studying
with this research group for the last five years, I think I would have
ended up not being an asset to my company."

The research group exacts a number of commitments from participants. One is a strict adherence to a "nine-to-five" schedule.
People beat a trail here, some from as far as 200 kilometers away,
and absence may lead to membership disqualification. Participation
was considered an obligation that communicated one's rigor and
depth of commitment. It seemed that my job was turning out to be
more than expected. I began feeling a growing responsibility
toward this story.

High-Diversity Research's Laboratory for Improvement

February 4 was the day of the regular monthly meeting.
This month's meeting at Shinano Specialty Equipment was
being conducted by Kurasawa. The posted schedule for the
day follows:

- Session 1 (9:05-9:30): Follow-up and Introduction
  - progress reports on homework from the previous meeting
  - explanation of materials utilized in the present research process

- Session 2 (9:35-9:50): Sekine's Topics
  - analyze processes to allow proficiency in free-flow line manufacturing
  - how to move from four- to two-person assembly operations

- Session 3 (9:50-14:00): On-site Research
- Session 4 (14:00-15:00): Recap
- Session 5 (15:00-16:00): "The Game"
- Session 6 (16:00-16:30): Office Report

Session 1

Materials are distributed, and Kazuhiro Itō from Shinano Specialty Equipment gives the report. High Diversity Research organizes two research meetings for every company. The first meeting is on eliminating waste and members give improvement suggestions for a selected process. This operation is intended to uncover areas of waste. After conducting the initial meeting at Shinano Specialty Equipment on January 6, the company was asked to report in the second meeting on the results of the suggested improvements.

Earlier requests had been made for (1) a calculation of the process time on the two free-flow lines and on the hand-operated line for motor assembly, (2) an assembly process chart for each separate line, and (3) a job roster listing all of the operators. A number of suggestions received for eliminating waste (such as constructing an automatic screwdriver, methods of suspending and preventing sway in adhesive applicators and screwdrivers, constructing an *andon* lamp that immediately lights up when trouble arises, creating a two-person line) already had been implemented with good results.

Improvements also progressed in constructing an adhesive application device for buff (mid-April); improving the nozzle of the adhesive applicator (mid-April), buff automatic press fitting (mid-February), constructing a roller conveyer for the free-flow line (mid-February) and so forth. Improvements under consideration include the following: moving to a spot heater on the hand-operated heater conveyor and rank-based job assignments for operators. All of these ideas had been suggested since the first meeting.

Following a question-and-answer session about Itō's report, many comment on the progress made so far.

Session 2

With Sekine's guidance, the themes are to analyze the processes to allow proficiency in free-flow line manufacturing and points to consider when moving from four- to two-person assembly operations.

Session 3

At 9:50, everyone goes to the workplace to conduct on-site research. Today's workplace is the same as the last meeting's — the free-flow and hand-operated assembly lines. Everybody watches the workers. One person takes notes and another, looking intently at a single point, is motionless. "This field is so different from my own, I'm at a complete loss. If they keep working like this, there won't be any room left for improvement!" The hand of the person taking notes moves quickly across the page as he speaks.

Session 4

Recap of the on-site research begins. Over four hours of study conducted at the workplace comes to an end, and each person is given a piece of paper on which to compose his formal suggestions for improvement. One man looks at his paper, nodding. Another stares intently at the ceiling. Yet another returns to the workplace to confirm a point and so on. Seriousness is etched across each face. The meeting room is tense and silent.

In other research groups, the instructor often places himself above those he instructs. Here, however, the instructor is also a member. He submits a paper each time just like the other members. Kurasawa expresses his admiration: "I have studied with a lot of different teachers in the past, but Sekine is the first instructor I've had who submits his own paper."

This research group does much more than simply listen to an instructor. Members submit formal suggestions for improvement and give reports, just as in a regular office. Speaking from the heart, Shioiri says, "It's really rough. I don't have any factory experience, but I have to work just like everyone else here." And according to Sekine, Shioiri is his "star" pupil.

Sekine is already finished writing. "Look at their faces," he quips. "These men work harder here than at their own companies!"

Dueling with Improvement Proposals

Session 5

Various research group highlights. The improvement duel called "The Game" begins. Its aim is to increase individual as opposed to group creativity. The five persons to give today's report are chosen by drawing straws.

Copies of the speakers' improvement proposals are distributed. Two-person assembly operation layout improvement, two-person process analysis, reducing the number of workers on a free-flow line, and so forth. The themes are similar, but the contents differ. A question-and-answer period follows each report. The discussion is concrete and specific, as those responsible for the workplace at Shinano Special Equipment are involved.

The last person to speak is Sekine. He states that Shinano Special Equipment must symbolize "fast action." He considers it incredible that in a mere month the company could have come this far toward implementing two-person assembly operations. He explains the fundamentals of precision parts assembly and then notes it is necessary to divide workers into two groups — those with people skills and those with equipment skills. He suggests dividing free-flow line process analysis into seven headings, points up the waste of moving inventory by hand in a two-person assembly line, and then raises the improvement question of using U-shaped lines.

The regular February meeting of the High-Diversity Research Group comes to a close. The meeting has lasted for eight hours, and the members — not to mention this reporter — are utterly exhausted.

Developing Improvement Professionals

As a link in the Varied Industries Exchange Group, the High Diversity Research Group is steadily growing. Shinano Specialty Equipment's Kazuhiro Itō, who enthusiastically opened the research group at his company, gave this off-the-cuff evaluation:

> *Since participating in the research group, our desire to improve has increased and the workplace has changed completely.*
>
> *From the perspective of locating waste and encouraging improvement techniques, the experience has been very valuable. It has*

served as a stimulus for our now very active improvement circle, and, taking up the research group's goal of waste elimination, we are launching a companywide rationalization campaign centering on a waste elimination strategy. Those who participate in these meetings develop an eye for improvement and return to their own companies with good, improvement-oriented habits.

Stressing the importance of selecting the right teacher, the assistant manager of the research group comments: "Since receiving guidance from Sekine, we members of the research group are swimming in improvement ideas. It's as if we can see for the first time."

The research group is composed of people from a wide variety of industries: computer components, automobile parts, women's apparel. The question often raised is whether such diversity might lead to an exchange of rather unsophisticated improvement ideas between dissimilar industries. Responding to this concern, Itō says,

I hear this a lot but it is just the opposite. It is precisely because our industries and jobs differ that we have such a wide variety of suggestions, all based upon our differing perspectives. When people from the printing or garment industries look at a company like mine — a manufacturer of precision motors — they often submit what appear to be impossible improvement proposals. Our first thought is "Oh, no . . ." When we actually try the proposals, however, they often work exceptionally well. Rather than such diversity being a detriment, our improvement vision is frequently enhanced when we are able to remove our subconscious blinders.

Office Enthusiasm Is a Key to Success

One factor that cannot be overlooked for the long life and success of the High-Diversity Research Group is the behind-the-scenes efforts of the central office called the Nagano Prefecture Integrated Guidance Center for Small- and Mid-Sized Businesses.

The last five years saw countless complications. Initially, there were enthusiastic companies and not-so-enthusiastic companies, making it difficult to conduct any kind of unified activity. Also, some felt that they were not experiencing results, in spite of their improvement goals. Therefore, in a "back to basics" move, the group focused its attention on bringing everyone up to the same level. To this end, the group made a change. Members cultivated simple, dirt-under-the-fingernails improvement techniques and immediately experienced a surge in activity levels.

According to Yamaguchi, the success of a research group of this kind hinges upon three keys:

1. Company executives must first recognize the necessity of a study group. The group must be used positively and in ways that are profitable to an enterprise. (In the High-Diversity Research Group, executives are invited to report on results at meetings and to join study groups.)
2. From a management perspective, it would be better to have a group structure in which regular employees — as opposed to "company representatives" — attend. It is difficult to make progress if participants rotate or take turns. A fixed group is also necessary to establish clearly defined responsibilities within the group.
3. It is important to select an instructor suited to the needs of the member companies. The research group relies upon a number of consultants to serve as instructors, although this has not always yielded favorable results.

When all is said and done, perhaps the most important thing is office enthusiasm. The office people were able to inspire the members and awaken in them the drive to succeed. They lent enthusiastic support and leadership to group activities. The secret of the High-Diversity Research Group's success is perhaps found in the words of Yamaguchi who said that if the office isn't "on fire," it is impossible for the research group to be "on fire."

CHAPTER FOURTEEN

JIT Puts People First

Just-in-time is a production method that puts people first. And even though management deals with people, JIT is actually "people-centered." By this we mean that it maximizes an individual's physical and mental capabilities — and sometimes even goes beyond.

For example, in such representative JIT methods as multiple process operations, standing operations, flow operations, *mizusumashi,* and visual control, the individual's ability is applied optimally and practically to tasks not suited to machines.

Shortly after Taiichi Ohno moved from Toyota Auto Body to Toyoda Gosei (the company within the Toyota Group that manufactures rubber and plastic components), a visitor to Toyoda Gosei asked the production supervisor what had been the biggest change since Ohno's arrival. He replied that Ohno said that "we didn't expect enough out of people, that it is a mistake to rely always and immediately on machines. He said that nothing was as marvelous as the ability of human beings and that mechanization and automation only become possible once you first make full use of human capabilities."

The supervisor then admitted that had he been asked, he would have said that "my tendency had been to lean heavily on the equipment-side of the equation. I put a lot of confidence in machines. But Ohno emphasized people, and I felt that I needed to make some fundamental changes in my thinking."

Automation and JIT

Toyota uses a steady multiprocess line. In this method, a number of machines are installed so that the goods are processed or the item is assembled with no more work than the press of a button — a so-called push-button operation.

Some authorities contend that there are three steps to workplace improvement: (1) operations improvement, (2) equipment improvement, and (3) process improvement. Further, they hold that these steps must be carried out in this order. However, when you maximally promote improvement and fully utilize the extent of human ability, you arrive at operations like the one described in the previous paragraph. Only when operations such as installing, attaching, and removing components are mechanized or robotized can total automation be achieved. The gradual buildup of compact and inexpensive automation is the kind of automation that is the basis of JIT.

JIT is directed toward automation and mechanization, however, factory automation and the like — which from the outset invest heavily in machines and robots — represent a completely different approach to equipment.

Thorough Management Training as Well

In a recent report on the Toyota management training system the training section chief stated, "We are not involved in systematic education and training. We are simply doing ordinary things practically and consistently. And, concerning training in the Toyota Production System, he said, "Because our job is manufacturing, thoroughness is our most serious consideration. The workplace is important, and management training includes hands-on factory experience."

The Toyota Production System's management course is intended to inculcate the knowledge and practical techniques that one must have as a manager in order to extend the system throughout the company. Lectures are geared toward department heads and section chiefs. Those in attendance are mainly those section chiefs who have recently transferred into a factory department or who have advanced through the departmental ranks. Incidentally, Toyota transfers from the administrative offices to factory departments occur as regularly as breakfast in the morning.

According to interviews with management candidates, the class imparts a general understanding of how the Toyota Production System works through an initial two-day seminar followed by a four-day and three-night training camp. At this camp, you "the trainee" actually enter the workplace to study improvement strategies. You are instructed by factory people about various processes and how to operate machinery and equipment. Following this general introduction, you are required to "improve the workplace" and report on the results of your "improvements." Four months later, another trial awaits — you must report before the executive-level factory superintendent on how you were able to improve the workplace entrusted to you. To complete the course, you must use this report and meet in conference with company management, such as the factory manager, department head, and section chief. At the present time, an even more practical course is being prepared for first-line supervisors.

That the Toyota Production System may be found throughout the administrative/technical and practical fields — the two major divisions of the Toyota Motors training system — speaks well of how much emphasis the company lays on this system.

Management Training — JIT Style

There is a feeling that we have come about as far as we can with management training. Following World War II, a variety of training methods such as Total Quality Control, Zero Defects, and the like were applied to small groups in rapid succession. However, none of these solved problems related to the factory. Only the Toyota Production System, however, has provided a method and a philosophy that can allow supervisors, by their own will, to challenge the ideal standards of quality, cost, and deadlines by using the people and machines placed at their disposals.

So says Gifu-area JIT consultant Hitoshi Yamada, who is a great admirer of Taiichi Ohno. Yamada suggests that supervisor training should be divided into trimesters, as follows:

First Trimester: Introduction. The course of study should be the Toyota Production System and it must begin with a teachable heart. If you do not throw off your previous ways of thinking and your previous methods of operation, you will be unable to understand the Toyota Production System.

Cleaning the bathroom, giving proper greetings as you enter and leave a room, looking cheerful when meeting others . . . For two days and one night, in order to break people free from their ruts, there is debate on these kinds of themes. In other words, give them "morale improvement training."

Next, give them a taste of actual practice. Give them concrete examples such as the characteristics of the assembly line's "one-piece flow," the machining line's "multiple process operation," and the finishing line's "set flow" and "flow press."

Yamada comments, "It's sort of like throwing a person who can't swim into the water. From this time on, we start searching for practical applications."

Second Trimester: Mastering the Toyota Production System. In the second trimester an individual's understanding of the methods involved in the Toyota Production System are deepened. In the workplace, a person will master methods such as the "pull" method, *kanban*, standard operations, and reducing setup time. The approach is one of "learning by doing."

Third Trimester: Putting the Toyota Production System into Practice. Students attempt to put the system into practice in their individual workplaces. During the three-month period, economizing labor and eliminating work in process are thoroughly studied for improvement ideas and the results investigated.

Yamada laments the present conditions in the workplace:

> Supervisors' abilities must include workplace leadership along with the ability to improve their own workplaces. Although management might say, "Let's give some direction to the employees," or "We must improve the workplace," this is often left up to the supervisors in the good name of "on-the-job" training, a practice undoubtedly followed in many businesses.
>
> Unless business leaders plant themselves in the workplace and demonstrate what a workplace capable of weathering the next generation should be like — as Taiichi Ohno did — their companies will not survive.

This is the declaration of a man who reportedly changed the production methods in both the wood manufacturing and apparel industries.

Listen and follow the directions of your **STATE AND LOCAL AUTHORITIES.**

IF YOU FEEL SICK, stay home. Do not go to work.

IF YOUR CHILDREN ARE SICK, keep them at home. Contact your medical provider.

IF YOU ARE AN OLDER PERSON, or have a serious underlying health condition, stay home and away from other people.

If someone in your household has **TESTED POSITIVE,** keep the entire household at home.

EVEN IF YOU ARE YOUNG, OR OTHERWISE HEALTHY, YOU ARE AT RISK AND YOUR ACTIVITIES CAN INCREASE THE RISK FOR OTHERS. IT IS CRITICAL THAT YOU DO YOUR PART TO SLOW THE SPREAD OF THE CORONAVIRUS.

Work or study **FROM HOME** whenever possible.

AVOID SOCIAL GATHERINGS in groups of more than 10 people.

Avoid eating or drinking at bars and restaurants — **USE PICKUP OR DELIVERY OPTIONS.**

AVOID DISCRETIONARY TRAVEL, shopping trips, and social visits.

DO NOT VISIT nursing homes or retirement or long-term care facilities unless to provide critical assistance.

ALWAYS PRACTICE GOOD HYGIENE:

• *Wash your hands, especially after touching any frequently used item or surface.*

• *Avoid touching your face.*

• *Sneeze or cough into a tissue, or the inside of your elbow.*

• *Disinfect frequently used items and surfaces as much as possible.*

CORONAVIRUS.GOV

SLOW THE SPREAD

PRESIDENT TRUMP'S CORONAVIRUS GUIDELINES FOR AMERICA

For more information, please visit

CORONAVIRUS.GOV

MARCH 16, 2020

THE WHITE HOUSE

CDC

Postal Customer

CHAPTER FIFTEEN

JIT Begins with an Awareness Revolution

JIT training is training in practical experience following four basic steps: (1) taking hold of basic thinking; (2) based upon that, giving guidance in methods and techniques; (3) trying those methods and techniques and ascertaining results; and (4) doing it yourself. The strong point of a system like JIT is its simplicity. The methods and techniques can be grasped easily by the worker on the job, and the results are likewise "in the hand" and easy to understand. Before JIT, no such simple, easily understood methods existed for management (or factory) improvement. There is little doubt, however, that the best training is in the workplace where anyone can try the methods and ascertain their results.

Let's look at a schedule of adjustments made by two companies during the period in which JIT was being introduced.

Yasuda Manufacturing

October 29, 1987: Kickoff

November 12, 1987: Field trip to Matsūra Machine

November 14, 1987: Field trip to Okamoto Machine Manufacturing

November 20, 1987: JIT Research Group

December 3, 1987: JIT Research Group

December 11, 1987: Meeting on awareness reform in the assembly area

December 17, 1987: JIT Research Group

December 19, 1987: Video produced on improving changeover times

January 5, 1988: JIT Research Group

January 19, 1988: Distribution of a small book of improvement examples from the workplace

January 27, 1988: JIT Research Group

January 30, 1988: Field trips to Gifu Auto Body and Enomoto Manufacturing

March 5, 1988: JIT Research Group

April 25, 1988: JIT Research Group

May 12, 1988: Question-and-answer meeting on public changeover of the assembly line

May 19, 1988: Public changeover of the assembly line

May 22, 1988: Regular meeting

June 1, 1988: Public changeover of the polishing process

June 2, 1988: Public changeover of the assembly line, changeover improvement group meeting

June 9, 1988: Setup improvement group meeting

June 10, 1988: Question-and-answer meeting

June 12, 1988: Public changeover of the assembly line

Shindengen Industries' Okabe Plant

Regarding the management structure:

1. Okabe Production System (OPS) general meeting (fourth Saturday of every month): policy approval, organization of activities, check on progress, revision of improvement plans

2. OPS committee meeting (second Saturday of every month): OPS development plans, plan drafting, prioritizing improvement plans, activity budgeting, selecting people to be responsible for carrying out OPS in the administrative offices

3. OPS promotion group meeting (once a week): shaping specific items to implement for OPS development, uncovering items for the improvement plan, selecting an OPS promotion representative for each department, in-house OPS public relations and morale building

September 4, 1987: Participation in an outside JIT seminar

September 4-5, 1987: Participation in Fujitsu's production management system study group

September 7, 1987: Kickoff meeting, distribution of the OPS plan

September 25, 1987: Field trip to Yamanashi Electronics

September 28, 1987: "Wellness Conference" at Manufacturing Section 2

September 30, 1987: Start of weekly production consultation meetings

October 1, 1987: First edition of "OPS News"

October 5, 1987: Inspection of the workplace by the OPS committee

October 8, 1987: OPS general meeting, OPS workplace diagnosis

October 9, 1987: Participation in outside JIT seminar

October 13, 1987: "One-piece flow" interim report

October 20, 1987: OPS general meeting (implemented "conference-while-standing")

October 23, 1987: QC diagnosis of a company affiliate, participation in a JIT lecture meeting

October 24, 1987: OPS workplace diagnosis
November 6, 1987: Participation in outside JIT seminar
November 9-10, 1987: Diagnosis by JIT Research
November 10, 1987: OPS general meeting, third issue of "OPS News"
November 14, 1987: OPS general meeting
November 18, 1987: Participation in Koma Electronics' study group
November 26, 1987: Field trip to Okamoto Machine Manufacturing
November 20, 1987: Fourth issue of "OPS News"

The preceding items illustrate two of the many ways companies have promoted JIT. Both companies actually used a variety of detailed and progressive methods. The importance to the campaign of office support might not be readily apparent by looking at this brief schedule. However, a campaign that does not build a person's improvement awareness is not really a campaign at all.

Introducing JIT in Three Steps

There are two approaches to management improvement. One method is a "special remedy" approach that seeks sudden, rapid results. The other is the "Chinese herbal medicine" approach that strives to slowly strengthen the constitution. Both methods are necessary for business and each may be used depending on the circumstances.

If one were to ask which approach JIT resembles more, it is undoubtedly the first. Although long-term care is better overall, in many specific instances, a single treatment is advisable.

The three steps for implementing JIT are:

Step #1: Change attitudes.

- Study materials such as magazines, books, videos, etc.
- Participate in training courses, seminars, and research groups.
- Encourage groups to observe and exchange information with more "advanced" companies or industries.
- Invite a consultant to lecture.

Because JIT challenges a company in new ways, there may be resistance or feelings of uncertainty might lead to difficulties. Constantly remind yourself of the need to break free of or change the present situation despite the difficulties such a change might bring.

- Develop a companywide campaign when possible.
- Frequently hold company research and study group meetings.

Sometimes there is a feeling that because this is the manufacturing department, there is no need to involve the office in our study or research groups. JIT cannot be promoted with such an attitude. The attitude must be that, when possible, the entire company needs to be involved in the improvement process. The themes that JIT addresses are widely applicable to both office and factory employees alike.

Step #2: Training to implement improvements.

- The company should have its own internal research and study groups
- Foster an "improvement person" though outside seminars, visits, etc.
- Receive on-site guidance from a consultant.

- Encourage exchanges with other workplaces.
- Encourage exchanges with other companies.

JIT improvement will not advance if a company relies on consultants. A consultant is not a company employee who has to come to work at your company every day.

A consultant is best thought of as a person to stimulate the company and give guidance concerning general company policy. No matter how talented the consultant is, it is nearly impossible for that person to master a company's product strategy and production methods. In numerous cases companies relied on consultants and were unable to follow through because the consultant's ideas were not enthusiastically received in the workplace. Regardless of the number of consultants or how good their advice is, the workplace attitude must change.

Skillfully drawing out the feelings of competitiveness within a company is an important part of implementing improvement strategies. The "public changeover" is conducted as if to say, "We have had successful changeover improvement. Everybody come, watch, learn well, and then take what is useful back to your own workplace. Imitate it so that you too might push ahead with workplace improvement." Workers begin to think, "Over there, they achieved those kinds of results just doing such-and-so. We can do better than that here!" In this way, the improvement circle widens.

An important point to mention here is the training of the factory-floor specialist who stands at the center of all this activity. Regardless of how much support the office gives, the most important consideration is the factory. JIT does not simply operate on the level of writing a report and "then you are done." A leader must become the center of group activity and the entire group must become independent. Only then is JIT real.

Step #3: Develop your own JIT specialist.

- Let the specialist study the company through tempo-rary transfers.
- Dispatch the specialist to other companies.
- Let the specialist study with a consulting firm.

Regardless of the kind of campaign initiated at a company, some regression will occur. Promotion time goes well, but once the campaign has ended, a company might experience "backsliding." It is important for a company to develop a specialist who will "advance the cause of JIT" in order to halt this trend. As with everything else, in JIT there are beginning and advanced levels. For improvements to progress as they should, you need an expert. Create a production research office like Toyota's, or assign a specialist to key workplaces. And don't forget to train people capable of giving JIT guidance to company affiliates and vendors.

Afterword

I was impressed by something that Lee Iacocca said in a recent newspaper column. He stressed that the U.S. manufacturing industry is putting all of its efforts into the money game and high-tech development; it is putting no energy into manufacturing. Yet, high technology is meaningless until it first finds a practical application in the workplace. And unless a country is a world industrial power, it is not a world power at all, he said. He concluded by saying that if its factories are not capable of competing worldwide, a nation is likewise unable to compete worldwide. American manufacturing industry is not really charting its course by the words of a man as influential as Iacocca. Only Wall Street is showing any signs of life activity.

This comment by Iacocca, president of Chrysler Corporation, is similar to the cries of an America suffering from a kind of disease. They would like to increase productivity. They would like to decrease production costs. They would like to produce goods that consumers are not going to bring claims against. They would like to develop products that are well-timed to the demands of customers. And on and on. It seems that Iacocca — who has been watching the Japanese auto industry to an annoying degree — has in this statement raised the voice of warning to U.S. enterprise.

I believe that Iacocca is a truly great manager. He also gives some very to-the-point suggestions on what should be done. Iacocca praises the courage of a young man with an MBA from Harvard, who might well have become rich on Wall Street by playing the money game. He instead has chosen to work as a floor manager in a Chrysler plant. Management that emphasizes the workplace — the front line for management activities — holds the winning card in manufacturing. This is not limited to the production workplace. The "treasure mountain" of improvement is in the workplace, and the treasure may only be discovered there.

One of my motivations in writing this book was to address the issue of why JIT — Japan's boast to the world — has not spread and developed to a greater degree domestically. So I wanted to focus on the workplace itself — with case studies, and about how the workplace had moved, how independent it had become, and how much energy it had put out.

Just-in-time — or JIT — was originated by Toyota; it is now more than ten years since it first made its debut at the end of the first oil shock. JIT has become well known as representative of Japanese-style management, not just in Japan but in Europe and the United States as well. But if you were to ask if JIT is really "alive" in Japan, no one would be able to answer with an unqualified "yes."

Why is this? Some sources contend that there is a problem with the method of implementation. When I was gathering facts at Toyota about JIT, I recall that JIT practitioners responded to this by saying that "the Toyota Production System is workplace technology." It would be no exaggeration to say that the workplace holds the very key to JIT success. While JIT is a management theory, at the same time, it is practicable technique.

Therefore, JIT functions may not be evident throughout company management, no matter how much a manager preaches JIT ideas. When this is the case, a supervisor or perhaps an outside consultant who can tie the manager's ideas to practical results becomes necessary. JIT as an idea is widely known in Europe and the West. Examples of practical application and results, however, are rare. Why is this also so? Because, unlike Japan, there is no power in — or foundation of independent management for — the workplace. In Japanese enterprises as well, workplaces have been losing the kind of "smarts," enthusiasm, and energy that were so conspicuous following the oil shock. This is regrettable. JIT set out as a more rational and efficient technology for the manufacture of goods. And persons in the workplace have the best ideas of the kinds of improvement needed to change the workplace.

JIT management — based upon the workplace — includes plenty of concepts and techniques that give priority to market needs. Some authorities contend that we have already entered the era where the manufacturing industry is the service industry. It is an era in which service is provided to a customer through the manufacture of goods. The needs of the marketplace are becoming more and more keen: increased variety of goods, low cost, improved quality, low delivery time, and so forth.

The reason that Japanese goods have such high quality and can be sold so inexpensively is of course because of a "top" or upper management that values quality and strives to create a pleasant work environment. Certainly people on the management level have worked hard to motivate their employees.

However, the biggest reason is the "bottom" — that is to say, those who work in the factories and who think harder and sweat more than any other people. They are the reason, and there is no other. No place in the entire world do people work or use their heads for the purpose of promoting business as in Japan. In a word, the Japanese workplace is high quality.

Many mistakes of European and U.S. companies are attributable to the thinking that when you automate, you no longer need operators. And so, the simple labor — which actually is not "simple labor" at all, but jobs that require a degree of intelligence — is often entrusted to unskilled or untrained laborers. It is a big mistake to think that the workplace will run by simply printing a couple of operations manuals to pass around. The modern workplace is not as simple as handbooks for employees in a fast-food restaurant chain.

A Glossary of Commonly Used JIT Terms

"JIT" is actually a synonym for the Toyota Production System. Many terms in use have been coined by Toyota. To firmly plant the idea that their production methods had changed, phrases were given meanings that contrasted with those held previously — or new words were coined. Following this difficult process, the words now are seen all over. Among these, *baka-yoke* (or "idiot-proof," related to *poka-yoke*) and *sarashikubi* ("a head on a gibbet") seem particularly harsh in Japanese. These words were selected intentionally, however, to leave a strong impression.

The following are some JIT words or terms commonly used at Toyota:

5S's.

In Japanese the 5S's are *seiri, seiton, seiketsu, seisō,* and *shitsuke* — or proper arrangement, orderliness, cleanliness, cleanup, and discipline. In JIT, the 5S's have logically come to serve as the foundation upon which all other workplace improvement is built. Traditionally, the 5S's were duties passively discharged at the end of the day before one left the workplace. In JIT, the 5S's are improvements as well as an aggressive technique that, when properly performed, reveal the opening through which other improvements might enter.

Andon.

A method utilized in *visual management*. A device (such as a red or green light bulb) that allows a manager or supervisor to see at a glance if the workplace is running properly. When an operator notices a problem in a machine, he or she presses a button. This lights up a lamp (or *andon*) that visually announces the problem so that it may be dealt with immediately.

Autonomation (jidoka).

Also referred to as "automation with a human touch," this term refers to machines equipped with simple automatic stop devices that prevent defective goods from being sent on to the next process. Thus, quality is improved without increasing machine supervision and a single operator can manage a number of machines at one time.

Configured Loading (nisugata).

Configured loading is necessitated by the use of the JIT principles of one-piece flow and small lot production, where knowing the exact number of units is important. In configured loading, a pallet will be designed and built to hold a fixed number of units or lot size.

Crying Wolf (okami shonen).

Let's assume you have inquired about the minimum number of parts necessary for inventory to avoid a stock-out and its associated work stoppage. When you make such an inquiry of each section in the long process from raw materials to assembly, some sections will "pad" their estimates out of fear that there will otherwise be a work stoppage. When such estimates are totaled, the resulting number is very inflated. In

JIT, overproduction is considered the worst of all possible wastes. The false (or inflated) estimate is called "crying wolf."

Cycle Time (saikeru taimu).
The amount of time necessary to produce an item (production capability).

Cycle time = hours of "up time" for the month (week, day, or hour) ÷ the production volume per month (week, day, or hour)

For example, if it takes 100 hours to make 2,000 items, cycle time is 0.05.

Defects (furyo).
There are various kinds of defects in the workplace (such as omitting a process, processing errors, process-setting errors, missing parts, and mistakenly combining the wrong parts). JIT presents a number of methods for eliminating defects, including flow production, multiprocess operations, *andon*, standard operations, *poka-yoke*, and autonomation.

Flow Production (nagare-ka).
Flow production is the intra-process placement of extra operations — not usually a part of the process — in order to eliminate idle-time waste. In Japanese, the term means the same thing as *nagare-zoku* (slang meaning to do two things at the same time) and refers to the operator's performance of a second operation during the idle time on a primary operation. In "flow press," for example, an assembly operation might be performed by an operator in between the times he or she operates the press machine.

Freeing Up Labor (hitobanashi).
This refers to a procedure used to increase productivity. There are two ways to free up (or economize) labor. The term used when one operator manages several machines of the

same type is "multiple equipment operation" or *tadai mochi*. When an operator manages several machines of different types, this is called "multiprocess operation" or *takotei mochi*.

Regardless of operation, it is impossible for a person operating multiple machines to stay with one machine from beginning to end. While one machine is operating, the person must be able to move to another machine to perform a changeover or the like. This system is what is meant by "freeing the laborer from the machine" or simply "freeing up labor" (*hitobanashi*). The fundamental idea behind this concept is "automation with a human touch" (or Toyota's term "autonomation").

Isolated Islands (hanare kojima).

When equipment is too far separated from the previous or subsequent process, it is impossible for the equipment operator to lend assistance to these processes, even when there is idle time. A process line layout that is based upon increases or decreases in production and that cannot be used for other operations is also called an "isolated island."

Kanban System (kanban hoshiki).

Kanban is the Japanese word for card, ticket, or sign. Here it is a production system in which you produce the needed amount of the needed goods at the time needed. Among the different types of *kanban* are "work order" *kanban* ("intraprocess" and "signal" *kanban*) and "withdrawal" (or "transport") *kanban*. When circulating *kanban*, it is important to keep their numbers low. Circulating too many at once can cause confusion.

Work order *kanban* are used for intra-process work orders in production lines — such as in the pressing and plastic fabrication processes — that do not need die exchanges, or in flow production lines. Inter-process withdrawal *kanban* indicate when a part should be pulled from the previous process. When the part to be withdrawn is being pulled from a subcontractor, the "subcontracted parts receiving" *kanban* is used.

The Toyota Production System is often called the "*Kanban* System." This is a misnomer, however, since the *kanban* system is only one of many methods used in production management.

Lead Time (riido taimu).

The time from raw material to finished product is called production lead time — and refers only the product needed, at the needed time, in the needed amount. It is important that the unit neither comes down the line too early nor too late. It is important to eliminate delay time.

Level Production (heijunka seisan).

The idea upon which the "pull" system operates; that is, manufacturing only as much product as has been sold. Here the marketing person minimizes sales fluctuations as much as possible so that there is little fluctuation in the demand upon the manufacturer. On the other hand, the manufacturer must also exercise resourcefulness in order to find ways to limit fluctuation.

Mistake-proofing (poka-yoke).

Mistakes resulting from fatigue or carelessness occur frequently in workplace operations. A *poka-yoke* is a simple device that stops defective goods from being sent on to the next process. *Poka-yoke* literally means "fool-proof."

Mixed Production (konryu seisan).

Mixed production means that a variety of products flows down the same line. Until recently, only one item was produced on a line at a time, and this in a sizable amount to ensure a large inventory. The movement toward one-piece (or small-lot) production brought with it a move toward mixing production as well.

Multiprocess Operation (takotei mochi).

Arranging the equipment in the processing sequence in order to allow a single operator to move from machine to machine and operate multiple processes. When an operator manages several machines of different types, the system is called "multiple process operation" (or "vertical multiprocessing [*tatemochi*])." On the other hand, when an operator manages several machines of the same type, it is called "multiple equipment operation (*tadai mochi*)" (or "horizontal multiprocessing" [*yokomochi*]).

One-Piece Flow Production (ikko nagashi or ikko zukuri).

In just-in-time, the ideal is to eliminate large product inventories and to manufacture or assemble from raw materials just the amount ordered by each individual customer. It is a production method in which items are produced individually rather than in large batches.

Operations Improvement, Equipment Improvement, Process Improvement (sagyo kaizen, setsubi kaizen, kotei kaizen).

Taiichi Ohno, the originator of the Toyota Production System, said that there is a proper order to improvement: operations improvement ➤ equipment improvement ➤ process improvement.

"Operations improvement" means you devise easier ways to use the equipment that you presently own. Next, "equipment improvement" means introducing new machines only when you have made maximum use of your present equipment and when it is no longer possible to pursue increased effectiveness without introducing new machines. If you introduce high-capacity machines from the outset, then operators will not have a firm grasp of what their jobs require, and the machines will end up running the operators, rather than the operators running the machines. "Making things extremely well by turning the process upside down" is process improvement. Process improvement means you deal with the problems of the workplace by using methods such as process linking, rearranging equipment so that it may be used in multiple processes, combining other types of processes, or making an overall layout change.

Personnel Rationalization (shojinka).

In Japanese, the term *shojinka* usually refers to personnel rationalization (that is, reduction) due to automation and mechanization. However, JIT stresses that there is no real "rationalization" of personnel. In this case, "rationalization" actually means to reduce the number of workers needed to perform a job. Because the Chinese characters used in the regular Japanese term mean "to terminate," a new Japanese word that sounds the same but uses different characters was coined. This new *shojinka* literally means "people lessening." This kind of personnel rationalization does not mean that you redetermine your quota and then terminate "unnecessary" personnel. Toyota distinguishes between (1) boldly reducing the number of persons working at a job by moving them to other areas as changes in production numbers warrant and (2) reducing the total number of personnel.

Process Linking (kotei no renzokuka).

To create a flow production demands that a process be connected as closely as possible with preceding and subsequent processes. In order to begin linking processes, it is necessary to first create U-shaped lines and then add various other kinds of improvements.

Public Display of Mistakes (sarashikubi).

The Japanese term literally means "head on a gibbet." In the old days, it was the custom to publicly display the heads of those who had been executed on a gibbet. This served as a warning to others to not make the same mistake. Likewise, when poor or defective units have been produced, they are displayed in a prominent place and everyone's attention is called to them in order to stop such defects from recurring. This policy is also intended to halt a regression in "improvement awareness."

Pull System (atokotei hikitori hoshiki).

Previously, the production of goods was based upon a plan that was made in advance. However, changes caused by fluctuations in the marketplace would result in confusion, large lots, inventory buildup, and so forth in the production plan. This process is called the "one-after-another" or "push" system. In JIT the reverse occurs — the subsequent process comes and "pulls" (or withdraws) the needed item from the preceding process when it is needed to manufacture goods. This process is called the "pull" system.

Quality Assurance (hinshitsu hosho).

Quality Assurance (QA) is one of the most important conditions necessary for the proper implementation of JIT. Should even one defect occur, JIT's "supreme directive" is to thoroughly investigate the cause and make whatever improvements necessary to ensure that it does not recur.

Small-Lot Production (sho-rotto seisan).

The production of a large quantity of the same item at one time is called "large-lot production." Manufacturing (ideally) one unit at a time, with the smallest number of goods possible being produced — allowing for leveled production — is called small-lot production.

Standard Operations (hyojun sagyo).

Standard operations refers to the thorough elimination of operation waste, the gathering together of only the most essential jobs, the creation of procedures that allow an operation to be performed repeatedly in the same way, and the coordinating of these with machines and operating times. At Toyota, it is not the staff but rather the supervisor who maintains and supervises standard operations. Being thoroughly acquainted with the workplace, the supervisor is also integral in effecting improvements.

Standing Operations (tachi sagyo).

In JIT, it is a fundamental principle that operators should stand while they work, whether engaged in machine processing operations or assembly work. Persons involved in multi-process operations should stand because they have to walk from machine to machine. However, because "baby-sitting operations" (in which the operator simply watches the machine work) are unpleasant, these workers must also move around frequently in order to stay alert. Although there is usually resistance when "sitting jobs" become "standing jobs," once people grow accustomed to it, they actually find standing more comfortable. It is also usual to experience a 20 percent increase in productivity when employees stand.

The Next Process Is the Customer (atokotei wa o-kyakusama).

No other expression in JIT is as significant as this one. In the "pull" system, the subsequent process comes to the preceding process to get the needed item, in the needed amount, at the needed time. JIT production is not organized properly if the preceding process fails to deliver as requested. For this reason, the preceding process must always do what the subsequent process says. This method illustrates that "the next process is the customer." Following this principle is difficult — and essential.

"I don't know if we can do that — we're so busy." "No way." "We'll try to get around to it — but you're not the only one placing orders." "I don't care how many times you ask! If we can't do it, we can't do it." A company where such comments are heard is not a company in which JIT has taken root.

U-shaped Line ("U" ji rain).

A "U-shaped line" is a production line in which the machines form a "U" shape. It is the line most suitable for multiprocess operations and one-piece flow because: (1) an operator can view the entire operation, allowing a single person to handle the sequence of operations from first to last process and to perform a quality check; (2) it allows for multiprocess operations with no "walking waste"; and (3) it allows workers to assist each other. Such merits are why the U-line is fast becoming the standard line shape.

Up Time (kadoritsu).

In standard Japanese, the term *kadoritsu* is written with the three Chinese characters for "ability," "movement," and "rate" or "ratio." The word literally means "ratio of movability." Toyota has coined a word, however, that shares the same sound as the original term but is written with different Chinese characters. The new Toyota word substitutes characters that mean "to earn money," "to make a profit," and "to work." The literal meaning of this new term is perhaps best translated as "ratio of revenue-producing operation," a term that indicates the ratio of how much time in a given period a machine is used to manufacture goods. The original term indicates the ratio of how much of the time — when you want to use the equipment — the equipment is functioning normally. Through maintenance inspection, JIT strives to have machines function efficiently 100 percent of the time; however, it doesn't matter how many good machines there are if they are only used when necessary.

Variable Personnel System (hitei insei).

A company must do away with questions such as "How many people does it take to do this job?" Also, jobs should not be decided by machine capacity or conveyer speed. The amount produced should be determined by the production requirements of the customer — and the appropriate number of people selected to produce that amount. A company should strive to reduce the number of employees needed for production as much as possible. If this system is adopted, the quota system will be discarded.

Visible Standard Operations (hyojun sagyo).

Derived from "standard operations" and coined by Toyota, this term means to make the proper execution of standard operations visibly demonstrable. The proper recording of the actual operation being performed is "visual standardization." Improvement begins when the actual situation is properly grasped.

Visual Management (me de miru kanri).

This general term refers to methods that enable a plant manager to spot things such as emergencies, problems, and the amount of an item in stock — all at a glance. For example, a person immediately knows how much product is in stock by looking quickly at an *andon* light or a production management board.

Waste (muda).

In manufacturing, waste is defined as production that only increases cost without adding value. Toyota has identified seven areas of waste: correcting defects, overproduction, fabrication, transport, inventory, movement, and idle time.

Whirligig Beetle (mizusumashi).

Operators in multiprocess operations such as the U-shaped line who stand in the middle of the line and repeat the same actions over and over are called whirligig beetles. The term also applies to transport workers who in order to head off shortages move quickly from process to process supplying parts. The term refers to the way in which the whirligig beetle moves rapidly from place to place on the top of a pond.

Selected Bibliography*

Akao, Yoji, ed. 1989. *Hoshin kanri: policy deployment for successful TQM.* Cambridge, MA: Productivity Press, 1991, English translation.

Akiyama, Kaneo. *Function analysis: systematic improvement of quality and performance.* Cambridge, MA: Productivity Press, 1991, English translation.

Aoki, Kameo. 1989. *Placement management: scientific arrangement and orderliness in the 5S's.* Cambridge, MA: Productivity Press, 1992, English translation.

Asahi, Tetsuro. Company study: Matsushita Electric. *Nikkan, Kōgyō Shimbun* 11 July 1988.

"A guide to industry-specific practical applications of the Toyota production system." *Kōgyō kanri.* Special Edition, May 1988.

Cusumano, Michael A. 1985. *The Japanese automobile industry: technology and management at Nissan and Toyota.* Cambridge, MA: Harvard University Press.

---

* These references have been selected by the author and the editor of the English translation.

Hirano, Hiroyuki. *JIT implementation manual: the complete guide to just-in-time manufacturing.* Cambridge, MA: Productivity Press, 1990, English translation.

Hirano, Hiroyuki, ed. "Speaking frankly: ninety questions and answers concerning JIT production." *Kōgyō kanri.* Special Edition, December 1987.

Hirano, Hiroyuki, and JIT Management Laboratory. 1987. *JIT factory revolution: a pictorial guide to factory design of the future.* Cambridge, MA: Productivity Press, 1988, English translation.

"The Hitachi production revolution." *Kōgyō kanri.* Special Edition, March 1980.

Iacocca, Lee. "Iacocca's corner: competitiveness begins with a fresh look at the industry." *Nihon keizai shimbun.* 4 April 1988.

Imai, Masaaki. 1986. *Kaizen: the key to Japan's competitive success.* New York: Random House.

Japan Human Relations Association, ed. 1990. *Kaizen teian 1: developing systems for continuous improvement through employee suggestions.* Cambridge, MA: Productivity Press, 1992, English translation.

Japan Management Association, ed. *Kanban and just-in-time at Toyota, revised.* Cambridge, MA: Productivity Press, 1989, English translation.

Kōgyō Kanri Henshubu, ed. 1986. *5S techniques.* Tokyo: Nikkan Kōgyō Shimbun.

"The man in the workplace: tirelessly increasing productivity by 50 percent." *Kōgyō kanri.* November 1984.

Monden, Yasuhiro, ed. 1992. *Cost management in the new manufacturing age: innovations in the Japanese automobile industry.* Cambridge, MA: Productivity Press.

Monden, Yasuhiro. 1983. *Toyota Production System.* Atlanta: Institute of Industrial Engineers.

Monden, Yasuhiro, and Sakurai, Michiharu, eds. 1990. *Japanese management accounting: a world class approach to profit management.* Cambridge, MA: Productivity Press.

Nagano Prefecture's Tashushoryo Production System Research Group. *Kōgyō kanri.* May 1984.

Nakai, Shigeyuki, ed. 1971. *Production management (Seisan kanri).* Tokyo: Diamond Publishing.

Nakajima, Seiichi. 1984. *Introduction to TPM: total productive maintenance.* Cambridge, MA: Productivity Press, 1988, English translation.

Nakajima, Seiichi, ed. 1985. *TPM development program: implementing total productive maintenance.* Cambridge, MA: Productivity Press, 1989, English translation.

Nikkan Kōgyō Shimbun, ed. 1987. *Poka-yoke: improving product quality by preventing defects.* Cambridge, MA: Productivity Press, 1988.

Ohno, Taiichi. 1978. *Toyota production system: beyond large-scale production.* Cambridge, MA: Productivity Press, 1988, English translation.

———. 1982. *Workplace management.* Cambridge, MA: Productivity Press, 1988, English translation.

Ohno, Taiichi with Mito, Setsuo. 1986. *Just-in-time for today and tomorrow.* Cambridge, MA: Productivity Press, 1988, English translation.

Pictorial: Sunwave's "akafuda strategy." *Kōgyō kanri.* October, 1984.

Sekine, Kenichi. *One-piece flow: cell design for transforming the production process.* Cambridge, MA: Productivity Press, 1992, English translation. [video set forthcoming]

Shingo, Shigeo. 1987. *Non-stock production: the Shingo system for continuous improvement.* Cambridge, MA: Productivity Press, 1988, English translation.

————. 1983. *A revolution in manufacturing: the SMED system.* Cambridge, MA: Productivity Press, 1985, English translation.

————. 1985. *The sayings of Shigeo Shingo: key strategies for plant improvement.* Cambridge, MA: Productivity Press, 1987, English translation.

————. 1991. *The Shingo production management system: improving process functions.* Cambridge, MA: Productivity Press, 1992, English translation.

————. 1980. *A study of the Toyota production system.* Cambridge, MA: Productivity Press, 1989, English translation.

————. 1985. *Zero quality control: source inspection and the poka-yoke system.* Cambridge, MA: Productivity Press, 1986, English translation.

Shinohara, Isao. 1985. *New production system: JIT crossing industry boundaries.* Cambridge, MA: Productivity Press, 1988, English translation.

Sugiyama, Tomō. 1981. *The improvement book: creating the problem-free workplace.* Cambridge, MA: Productivity Press, 1989, English translation.

————. 1984. *Methods of cultivating improvement strategies (Kaizen hasso no sodatekata).* Tokyo: Nikkan Kōgyō Shimbun.

Tamagata Prefecture: Yonekawa System Research Group. *Kōgyō kanri.* Special Issue No. 2, September 1985.

"The Toyota production system's 'new wave'." *Kōgyō kanri.* Special Edition, May 1985.

Yamada, Hitoshi. 1987. *Complete dictionary of the Toyota production system.* Tokyo: Nikkan Kōgyō Shimbun.

Yasuda, Yuzo. 1989. *40 years, 20 million ideas: the Toyota suggestion system.* Cambridge, MA: Productivity Press, 1991, English translation.

About the Author

Ichiro Majima has worked for Nikkan Kōgyō Shimbun (NKS) in Tokyo since 1963. He began as a reporter for a monthly magazine related to machine processing, civil engineering, and metal materials. In 1981 he was promoted to editor-in-chief of the trade journal *Press Working*. Two years later he was named editor-in-chief of *Factory Management* (*Kōgyō kanri*). During his tenure, he introduced into this premier Japanese manufacturing journal regular coverage of such topics as just-in-time, worksite improvement, and factory rationalization campaigns. In 1989, Mr. Majima was again promoted, this time to the post of managing editorial director of NKS's publishing bureau. Since 1990, he has also served as deputy bureau chief. The author was born in 1938.

Index

More Books On Manufacturing Process Improvement

Productivity Press publishes and distributes materials on continuous improvement in productivity, quality, customer service, and the creative involvement of all employees. Many of our products are direct source materials from Japan that have been translated into English for the first time and are available exclusively from Productivity. Supplemental products and services include newsletters, conferences, seminars, in-house training and consulting, audio-visual training programs, and industrial study missions. Call 1-800-394-6868 for our free book catalog.

The Battle to Stay Competitive
Changing the Traditional Workplace
The Delco Moraine NDH Story

Charles Birkholz and Jim Villella

This inspiring and quick-reading book tells the story of one company's non-traditional response to increased competition and threatened market share. It recalls in vivid detail the changes undertaken by Delco Moraine NDH, General Motor's Brake Systems Division, that earned them a position as a world class supplier of automotive components. This case study documents the company's efforts to strengthen their competitiveness through synchronous manufacturing — the coordination of resources (man, machine, and materials) to eliminate waste. The personal accounts of Charles Birkholz and Jim Villella, key players in the company's evolution, describe the various efforts at the floor level to change the standards and performance of their division of the decidedly traditional GM company.

ISBN 0-915299-96-8 / 112 pages / $12.00 paper / Order code BATTLE-B207

JIT Factory Revolution
A Pictorial Guide to Factory Design of the Future
Hiroyuki Hirano / JIT Management Library

Here is the first-ever encyclopedic picture book of JIT. With 240 pages of photos, cartoons, and diagrams, this unprecedented behind-the-scenes look at actual production and assembly plants shows you exactly how JIT looks and functions. It shows you how to set up each area of a JIT plant and provides hundreds of useful ideas you can implement. If you've made the crucial decision to run production using JIT and want to show your employees what it's all about, this book is a must. The photographs, from Japanese production and assembly plants, provide vivid depictions of what work is like in a JIT environment. And the text, simple and easy to read, makes all the essentials crystal clear.
ISBN 0-915299-44-5 / 227 pages / $49.95 / Order code JITFAC-B207

JIT Implementation Manual
The Complete Guide to Just-In-Time Manufacturing
Hiroyuki Hirano

Encyclopedic in scope and written by a top international consultant, this comprehensive manual provides the JIT professional with the answer to virtually any JIT problem. It shows multiple options for handling every stage of implementation, is appropriate to all factory settings, and covers JIT concepts, techniques, and tools, and includes hundreds of illustrations and JIT management forms.
1000+ pages in 2 volumes / $2500.00 / Order HIRJIT B207

IE for the Shop Floor 1
Productivity Through Process Analysis
Junichi Ishiwata

Industrial engineering (IE) lies at the heart of many of the most significant waste-reducing and quality-adding improvements in the manufacturing industry. This new book makes IE techniques accessible to managers, supervisors, and shop floor managers. It provides an overview of the methodologies of process analysis and includes abundant examples, case studies, illustrations, and sample process analysis charts and flow diagrams.
ISBN 0-915299-82-8 / 208 pages / $39.95 / Order code SHOPF1-B207

IE For The Shop Floor 2
Productivity Through Motion Study
Kenichiro Kato

This second volume in our new set on Industrial Engineering techniques for non-engineers focuses on the outstanding gains to be made in productivity and quality through the practice of motion study. It traces the historical development of motion study, describes how it can be used to analyze everyday tasks and factory operations, outlines various types of motion study, and discusses the therblig at length.
ISBN 1-56327-000-5 / 224 pages / $39.95 / Order SHOPF2-B207

Kanban and Just-In-Time at Toyota
Management Begins at the Workplace (rev.)
Japan Management Association (ed.), David J. Lu (translator)

Based on seminars developed by Taiichi Ohno and others at Toyota for their major suppliers, this book is the best practical introduction to Just-In-Time available. Now in a newly expanded edition, it explains every aspect of a "pull" system in clear and simple terms — the underlying rationale, how to set up the system and get everyone involved, and how to refine it once it's in place. A groundbreaking and essential tool for companies beginning JIT implementation.
ISBN 0-915299-48-8 / 224 pages / $39.95 / Order code KAN-B207

Canon Production System
Creative Involvement of the Total Workforce
compiled by the Japan Management Association

A fantastic success story! Canon set a goal to increase productivity by three percent per month — and achieved it! The first book-length case study to show how to combine the most effective Japanese management principles and quality improvement techniques into one overall strategy that improves every area of the company on a continual basis. Shows how the major QC tools are applied in a matrix management model.
ISBN 0-915299-06-2 / 256 pages / $39.95 / Order code CAN-B207

20 Keys to Workplace Improvement
Iwao Kobayashi

This easy-to-read introduction to the "20 keys" system presents an integrated approach to assessing and improving your company's competitive level. The book focuses on systematic improvement through five levels of achievement in such primary areas as industrial housekeeping, small group activities, quick changeover techniques, equipment maintenance, and computerization. A scoring guide is included, along with information to help plan a strategy for your company's world class improvement effort.
ISBN 0-915299-61-5 / 264 pages / $39.95 / Order code 20KEYS-B207

Co-makership
The New Supply Strategy for Manufacturers
Giorgio Merli

A cornerstone in the foundation of any world-class operation is strong supplier relations. A company that establishes partnerships with its suppliers opens the door to competitive advantage in terms of cost, service, quality, innovation, and time. International consultant Giorgio Merli describes the cultural evolution and the practical techniques necessary for a co-makership relationship to thrive. This approach is a prerequisite for product-planning systems, QFD, concurrent engineering, and other practices of world-class manufacturing.
ISBN 0-915299-84-4 / 224 pages / $39.95 / Order code COMAKE-B207

Total Manufacturing Management
Production Organization for the 1990s
Giorgio Merli

One of Italy's leading consultants discusses the implementation of Just-In-Time and related methods (including QFD and TPM) in Western corporations. The author does not approach JIT from a mechanistic orientation aimed simply at production efficiency. Rather, he discusses JIT from the perspective of industrial strategy and as an overall organizational model. Here's a sophisticated program for organizational reform that shows how JIT can be applied even in types of production that have often been neglected in the West, including custom work.
ISBN 0-915299-58-5 / 344 pages / $39.95 / Order code TMM-B207

Productivity Press, Inc., Dept. BK, P.O. Box 3007, Cambridge, MA 02140 1-800-394-6868

Continuous Improvement in Operations
A Systematic Approach to Waste Reduction
Alan Robinson (ed.)

Now one handy book brings you the world's most advanced thinking on Just-In-Time, *kaizen*, Total Employee Involvement, and Total Productive Maintenance. Here in one volume is a compendium of materials from our best-selling classics by world-famous manufacturing experts. A lengthy introduction integrates the developments of these manufacturing gurus within a twofold theme the elimination of invisible waste and the creation of a work environment that welcomes and institutes employee's ideas. It's a perfect book for your study groups and improvement teams.
ISBN 0-915299-51-8 / 416 pages / $34.95 / Order ROB2C-B207

One-Piece Flow
Cell Design for Transforming the Production Process
Kenichi Sekine

By reconfiguring your traditional assembly lines into production cells based on one-piece flow, you can drastically reduce your lead time, manpower requirements, and number of defects. Kenichi Sekine examines the basic principles of process flow building, then offers detailed case studies of how various industries designed unique one-piece flow systems (parallel, L-shaped, and U-shaped floor plans) to meet their particular needs.
ISBN 0-915299-33-X / 392 pages / $85.00 / Order code 1PIECE-xx

A Revolution in Manufacturing
The SMED System
Shigeo Shingo, translated by Andrew P. Dillon

SMED (Single-Minute Exchange of Die), or quick changeover techniques, is the single most powerful tool for Just-In-Time production. Written by the industrial engineer who developed SMED for Toyota, the book contains hundreds of illustrations and photographs, as well as twelve chapter-length case studies. Here are the most complete and detailed instructions available anywhere for transforming a manufacturing environment to speed up production (Shingo's average setup time reduction is an astounding 98 percent) and make small-lot inventories feasible.
ISBN 0-915299-03-8 / 383 pages / $75.00 / Order code SMED-B207

A Study of the Toyota Production System
From an Industrial Engineering Viewpoint (rev.)
Shigeo Shingo

Here is Dr. Shingo's classic industrial engineering rationale for the priority of process-based over operational improvements for manufacturing. He explains the basic mechanisms of the Toyota production system in a practical and simple way so that you can apply them in your own plant. This book clarifies the fundamental principles of JIT including levelling, standard work procedures, multi-machine handlng, and more.
ISBN 0-915299-17-8 / 294 pages / $44.95 / Order code STREV-B207

Non-Stock Production
The Shingo System for Continuous Improvement
Shigeo Shingo

Shingo, whose work at Toyota provided the foundation for JIT, teaches how to implement non-stock production in your JIT manufacturing operations. The culmination of his extensive writings on efficient production management and continuous improvement, this book is an essential companion volume to his other landmark books on key elements of JIT, including SMED and Poka-Yoke.
ISBN 0-915299-30-5 / 480 pages / $85.00 / Order code NON-B207

The Shingo Production Management System
Improving Process Functions
Shigeo Shingo

Shigeo Shingo sparked a revolution in the manufacturing industry with tools such as the Single-Minute Exchange of Die, Non-Stock Production, and Zero Quality Control. Here, in his long-awaited and final book, he ties it all together to give us a comprehensive system for the improvement of production functions. This powerful book's broad scope encompasses such diverse topics as Value Engineering, CAD/CAM techniques, and information management. If you've never read Shingo, this book will give you an overview of his brilliant concepts and how they interrelate. If you are familiar with his genius, you'll find in this book a much-needed network of his ideas.
ISBN 0-915299-52-6 / 272 pages / $49.95 / Order code SHPMS-B207

Productivity Press, Inc., Dept. BK, P.O. Box 3007, Cambridge, MA 02140 1-800-394-6868

Also From Productivity

Achieving One-Piece Flow through Cell Design
Kenichi Sekine

Visit a factory using one-piece flow production and you'll see its advantages in time, quality, and manpower. This video training series uses live action footage, graphics, and case examples to bring you into companies for a first-hand look at cell design implementation. It is a powerful, efficient, and low-cost way to enlighten your entire workforce in the techniques of cell design. Video set comes with three videotapes, one facilitator's reference guide, one application workbook, and one copy of **One-Piece Flow: Cell Design for Transforming the Production Process**.
ISBN 1-56327-001-3 / $1,495.00 / Order code VAPF1/2-B207

Productivity Press, Inc., Dept. BK, P.O. Box 3007, Cambridge, MA 02140 1-800-394-6868

COMPLETE LIST OF TITLES FROM PRODUCTIVITY PRESS

Akao, Yoji (ed.). **Quality Function Deployment: Integrating Customer Requirements into Product Design**
ISBN 0-915299-41-0 / 1990 / 387 pages / $ 85.00 / order code QFD-B207

Akiyama, Kaneo. **Function Analysis: Systematic Improvement of Quality and Performance**
ISBN 0-915299-81-X / 1991 / 288 pages / $59.95 / order code FA-B207

Asaka, Tetsuichi and Kazuo Ozeki (eds.). **Handbook of Quality Tools: The Japanese Approach**
ISBN 0-915299-45-3 / 1990 / 336 pages / $65.00 / order code HQT-B207

Belohlav, James A. **Championship Management: An Action Model for High Performance**
ISBN 0-915299-76-3 / 1990 / 265 pages / $29.95 / order code CHAMPS-B207

Birkholz, Charles and Jim Villella. **The Battle to Stay Competitive: Changing the Traditional Workplace**
ISBN 0-915299-96-8 / 1991 / 110 pages paper / $12.00 /order code BATTLE-B207

Christopher, William F. **Productivity Measurement Handbook**
ISBN 0-915299-05-4 / 1985 / 680 pages / $150.00 / order code PMH-B207

D'Egidio, Franco. **The Service Era: Leadership in a Global Environment**
ISBN 0-915299-68-2 / 1990 / 165 pages / $29.95 / order code SERA-B207

Ford, Henry. **Today and Tomorrow**
ISBN 0-915299-36-4 / 1988 / 286 pages / $24.95 / order code FORD-B207

Fukuda, Ryuji. **CEDAC: A Tool for Continuous Systematic Improvement**
ISBN 0-915299-26-7 / 1990 / 144 pages / $54.95 / order code CEDAC-B207

Fukuda, Ryuji. **Managerial Engineering: Techniques for Improving Quality and Productivity in the Workplace** (rev.)
ISBN 0-915299-09-7 / 1986 / 208 pages / $44.95 / order code ME-B207

Gotoh, Fumio. **Equipment Planning for TPM: Maintenance Prevention Design**
ISBN 0-915299-77-1 / 1991 / 320 pages / $85.00 / order code ETPM-B207

Greif, Michel. **The Visual Factory: Building Participation Through Shared Information**
ISBN 0-915299-67-4 / 1991 / 320 pages / $54.95 / order code VFAC-B207

Hatakeyama, Yoshio. **Manager Revolution! A Guide to Survival in Today's Changing Workplace**
ISBN 0-915299-10-0 / 1986 / 208 pages / $24.95 / order code MREV-B207

Hirano, Hiroyuki. **JIT Factory Revolution: A Pictorial Guide to Factory Design of the Future**
ISBN 0-915299-44-5 / 1989 / 227 pages / $49.95 / order code JITFAC-B207

Productivity Press, Inc., Dept. B207, P.O. Box 3007, Cambridge, MA 02140 1-800-274-9911

Hirano, Hiroyuki. **JIT Implementation Manual: The Complete Guide to Just-In-Time Manufacturing**
ISBN 0-915299-66-6 / 1990 / 1006 pages / $2500.00 / order code HIRJIT-B207

Horovitz, Jacques. **Winning Ways: Achieving Zero-Defect Service**
ISBN 0-915299-78-X / 1990 / 165 pages / $24.95 / order code WWAYS-B207

Ishiwata, Junichi. **IE for the Shop Floor: Productivity Through Process Analysis**
ISBN 0-915299-82-8 / 1991 / 208 pages / $39.95 / order code SHOPF1-B207

Japan Human Relations Association (ed.). **The Idea Book: Improvement Through TEI (Total Employee Involvement)**
ISBN 0-915299-22-4 / 1988 / 232 pages / $54.95 / order code IDEA-B207

Japan Human Relations Association (ed.). **The Service Industry Idea Book: Employee Involvement in Retail and Office Improvement**
ISBN 0-915299-65-8 / 1991 / 294 pages / $49.95 / order code SIDEA-B207

Japan Management Association (ed.). **Kanban and Just-In-Time at Toyota: Management Begins at the Workplace** (rev.), Translated by David J. Lu
ISBN 0-915299-48-8 / 1989 / 224 pages / $39.95 / order code KAN-B207

Japan Management Association and Constance E. Dyer. **The Canon Production System: Creative Involvement of the Total Workforce**
ISBN 0-915299-06-2 / 1987 / 251 pages / $39.95 / order code CAN-B207

Jones, Karen (ed.). **The Best of TEI: Current Perspectives on Total Employee Involvement**
ISBN 0-915299-63-1 / 1989 / 502 pages / $199.00 / order code TEI-B207

JUSE. **TQC Solutions: The 14-Step Process**
ISBN 0-915299-79-8 / 1991 / 416 pages / 2 volumes / $120.00 / order code TQCS-B207

Kanatsu, Takashi. **TQC for Accounting: A New Role in Companywide Improvement**
ISBN 0-915299-73-9 / 1991 / 244 pages / $45.00 / order code TQCA-B207

Karatsu, Hajime. **Tough Words For American Industry**
ISBN 0-915299-25-9 / 1988 / 178 pages / $24.95 / order code TOUGH-B207

Kato, Kenichiro. **I.E. for the Shop FLoor: Productivity Through Motion Study**
ISBN 1-56327-000-5 / 1991 / 224 pages / $39.95 / order code SHOPF2-B207

Kaydos, Will. **Measuring, Managing, and Maximizing Performance**
ISBN 0-915299-98-4 / 1991 / 304 pages / $39.95 / order code MMMP-B207

Kobayashi, Iwao. **20 Keys to Workplace Improvement**
ISBN 0-915299-61-5 / 1990 / 264 pages / $39.95 / order code 20KEYS-B207

Lu, David J. **Inside Corporate Japan: The Art of Fumble-Free Management**
ISBN 0-915299-16-X / 1987 / 278 pages / $24.95 / order code ICJ-B207

Maskell, Brian H. **Performance Measurement for World Class Manufacturing: A Model for American Companies**
ISBN 0-915299-99-2 / 1991 / 448 pages / $54.95 / order code PERFM-B207

Productivity Press, Inc., Dept. B207, P.O. Box 3007, Cambridge, MA 02140 1-800-274-9911

Merli, Giorgio. **Co-makership: The New Supply Strategy for Manufacturers**
ISBN 0-915299-84-4 / 1991 / 224 pages / $39.95 / order code COMAKE-B207

Merli, Giorgio. **Total Manufacturing Management: Production Organization for the 1990s**
ISBN 0-915299-58-5 / 1990 / 304 pages / $39.95 / order code TMM-B207

Mizuno, Shigeru (ed.). **Management for Quality Improvement: The 7 New QC Tools**
ISBN 0-915299-29-1 / 1988 / 324 pages / $65.00 / order code 7QC-B207

Monden, Yasuhiro and Michiharu Sakurai (eds.). **Japanese Management Accounting: A World Class Approach to Profit Management**
ISBN 0-915299-50-X / 1990 / 568 pages / $65.00 / order code JMACT-B207

Nachi-Fujikoshi (ed.). **Training for TPM: A Manufacturing Success Story**
ISBN 0-915299-34-8 / 1990 / 272 pages / $65.00 / order code CTPM-B207

Nakajima, Seiichi. **Introduction to TPM: Total Productive Maintenance**
ISBN 0-915299-23-2 / 1988 / 149 pages / $45.00 / order code ITPM-B207

Nakajima, Seiichi. **TPM Development Program: Implementing Total Productive Maintenance**
ISBN 0-915299-37-2 / 1989 / 428 pages / $95.00 / order code DTPM-B207

Nikkan Kogyo Shimbun, Ltd./Factory Magazine (ed.). **Poka-yoke: Improving Product Quality by Preventing Defects**
ISBN 0-915299-31-3 / 1989 / 288 pages / $65.00 / order code IPOKA-B207

Nikkan Kogyo Shimbun/Esme McTighe (ed.). **Factory Management Notebook Series: Mixed Model Production**
ISBN 0-915299-97-6 / 1991 / 184 pages / $95.00 / order code N1-MM-B207

Nikkan Kogyo Shimbun/Esme McTighe (ed.). **Factory Management Notebook Series: Visual Control Systems**
ISBN 0-915299-54-2 / 1991 / 194 pages / $95.00 / order code N1-VCS-B207

Nikkan Kogyo Shimbun/Esme McTighe (ed.). **Factory Management Notebook Series: Autonomation/ Automation**
ISBN 0-56327-002-1 / 1991 / 200 pages / $95.00 / order code N1-AA-B207

Ohno, Taiichi. **Toyota Production System: Beyond Large-Scale Production**
ISBN 0-915299-14-3 / 1988 / 162 pages / $42.95 / order code OTPS-B207

Ohno, Taiichi. **Workplace Management**
ISBN 0-915299-19-4 / 1988 / 165 pages / $39.95 / order code WPM-B207

Ohno, Taiichi and Setsuo Mito. **Just-In-Time for Today and Tomorrow**
ISBN 0-915299-20-8 / 1988 / 208 pages / $39.95 / order code OMJIT-B207

Perigord, Michel. **Achieving Total Quality Management: A Program for Action**
ISBN 0-915299-60-7 / 1991 / 384 pages / $49.95 / order code ACHTQM-B207

Psarouthakis, John. **Better Makes Us Best**
ISBN 0-915299-56-9 / 1989 / 112 pages / $16.95 / order code BMUB-B207

Productivity Press, Inc., Dept. B207, P.O. Box 3007, Cambridge, MA 02140 1-800-274-9911

Robinson, Alan. **Continuous Improvement in Operations: A Systematic Approach to Waste Reduction**
ISBN 0-915299-51-8 / 1991 / 416 pages / $34.95 / order code ROB2-C-B207

Robson, Ross (ed.). **The Quality and Productivity Equation: American Corporate Strategies for the 1990s**
ISBN 0-915299-71-2 / 1990 / 558 pages / $29.95 / order code QPE-B207

Shetty, Y.K and Vernon M. Buehler (eds.). **Competing Through Productivity and Quality**
ISBN 0-915299-43-7 / 1989 / 576 pages / $39.95 / order code COMP-B207

Shingo, Shigeo. **Non-Stock Production: The Shingo System for Continuous Improvement**
ISBN 0-915299-30-5 / 1988 / 480 pages / $85.00 / order code NON-B207

Shingo, Shigeo. **A Revolution In Manufacturing: The SMED System**, Translated by Andrew P. Dillon
ISBN 0-915299-03-8 / 1985 / 383 pages / $75.00 / order code SMED-B207

Shingo, Shigeo. **The Sayings of Shigeo Shingo: Key Strategies for Plant Improvement**, Translated by Andrew P. Dillon
ISBN 0-915299-15-1 / 1987 / 208 pages / $44.95 / order code SAY-B207

Shingo, Shigeo. **A Study of the Toyota Production System from an Industrial Engineering Viewpoint**
ISBN 0-915299-17-8 / 1989 / 293 pages / $44.95 / order code STREV-B207

Shingo, Shigeo. **Zero Quality Control: Source Inspection and the Poka-yoke System**, Translated by Andrew P. Dillon
ISBN 0-915299-07-0 / 1986 / 328 pages / $75.00 / order code ZQC-B207

Shinohara, Isao (ed.). **New Production System: JIT Crossing Industry Boundaries**
ISBN 0-915299-21-6 / 1988 / 224 pages / $39.95 / order code NPS-B207

Sugiyama, Tomo. **The Improvement Book: Creating the Problem-Free Workplace**
ISBN 0-915299-47-X / 1989 / 236 pages / $54.95 / order code IB-B207

Suzue, Toshio and Akira Kohdate. **Variety Reduction Program (VRP): A Production Strategy for Product Diversification**
ISBN 0-915299-32-1 / 1990 / 164 pages / $59.95 / order code VRP-B207

Tateisi, Kazuma. **The Eternal Venture Spirit: An Executive's Practical Philosophy**
ISBN 0-915299-55-0 / 1989 / 208 pages/ $19.95 / order code EVS-B207

Yasuda, Yuzo. **40 Years, 20 Million Ideas: The Toyota Suggestion System**
ISBN 0-915299-74-7 / 1991 / 210 pages / $39.95 / order code 4020-B207

Productivity Press, Inc., Dept. B207, P.O. Box 3007, Cambridge, MA 02140 1-800-274-9911

Audio-Visual Programs

Japan Management Association. **Total Productive Maintenance: Maximizing Productivity and Quality**
ISBN 0-915299-46-1 / 167 slides / 1989 / $799.00 / order code STPM-B207
ISBN 0-915299-49-6 / 2 videos / 1989 / $799.00 / order code VTPM-B207

Shingo, Shigeo. **The SMED System**, Translated by Andrew P. Dillon
ISBN 0-915299-11-9 / 181 slides / 1986 / $799.00 / order code S5-B207
ISBN 0-915299-27-5 / 2 videos / 1987 / $799.00 / order code V5-B207

Shingo, Shigeo. **The Poka-yoke System**, Translated by Andrew P. Dillon
ISBN 0-915299-13-5 / 235 slides / 1987 / $799.00 / order code S6-B207
ISBN 0-915299-28-3 / 2 videos / 1987 / $799.00 / order code V6-B207

Returns of AV programs willl be accepted for incorrect or damaged shipments only.

TO ORDER: Write, phone, or fax Productivity Press, Dept. BK, P.O. Box 3007, Cambridge, MA 02140, phone 1-800-274-9911, fax 617-864-6286. Send check or charge to your credit card (American Express, Visa, MasterCard accepted).

U.S. ORDERS: Add $5 shipping for first book, $2 each additional for UPS surface delivery. CT residents add 8% and MA residents 5% sales tax. For each AV program that you order, add $5 for programs with 1 or 2 tapes, and $12 for programs with 3 or more tapes.

INTERNATIONAL ORDERS: Write, phone, or fax for quote and indicate shipping method desired. Pre-payment in U.S. dollars must accompany your order (checks must be drawn on U.S. banks). When quote is returned with payment, your order will be shipped promptly by the method requested.

NOTE: Prices subject to change without notice.

113ge9